In the Matter of
J. Robert Oppenheimer

IN THE MATTER OF
J. Robert Oppenheimer

Politics, Rhetoric, and Self-Defense

RACHEL L. HOLLOWAY

PRAEGER

Westport, Connecticut
London

Library of Congress Cataloging-in-Publication Data

Holloway, Rachel L.
    In the matter of J. Robert Oppenheimer : politics, rhetoric, and
self-defense / Rachel L. Holloway.
      p. cm.
    Includes bibliographical references and index.
    ISBN 0-275-94429-8 (alk. paper)
    1. Oppenheimer, J. Robert, 1904-1967—Trials, litigations, etc.
    2. Hydrogen bomb—History. 3. Loyalty-security program, 1947-
    4. United States—Politics and government—1953-1961.
    5. Physicists—United States—Biography. 6. Oppenheimer, J. Robert,
    1904-1967. I. Title.
    QC16.062H65   1993
    530 '.092—dc20   92-35350
    [B]

British Library Cataloguing in Publication Data is available.

Library of Congress Catalog Card Number: 92-35350
ISBN: 0-275-94429-8

First published in 1993

Praeger Publishers, 88 Post Road West, Westport, CT 06881
An imprint of Greenwood Publishing Group, Inc.

Printed in the United States of America

The paper used in this book complies with the
Permanent Paper Standard issued by the National
Information Standards Organization (Z39.48-1984).

10 9 8 7 6 5 4 3 2 1

Contents

Figures

Preface

As students wait in my office, they often amuse themselves by studying the various items hanging on the walls. Invariably, they read a particular "Bloom County" cartoon strip several times and look increasingly perplexed. They look at it and then at me and then back at the cartoon again. The especially curious ones ask for an interpretation. The cartoon shows an adoring young girl running toward Oliver Wendell Jones, the child genius. She says, "You! You're the fellow who built this wild little atom bomb, aren't you?!" She continues: "Some of us happen to find men who make nuclear weapons simply irresistible." I explain to the curious onlookers that I'm a scientist "wanna-be" and that the "father of the atomic bomb" captured my attention long ago.[1]

My interest in J. Robert Oppenheimer started in high school. For once I was pleased that my parents watched PBS, because the network's series about Oppenheimer's life and his security hearing raised questions about a world I'd taken for granted. As a member of a generation that grew up with a nuclear arms race, security based on mutual assured destruction, and détente, I was intrigued by the scientific work that had created the political backdrop for my life. For the first time I began to think of the Cold War, not as the inevitable progress of science, but as a political decision. For whatever reason, dissatisfaction with analyses of Oppenheimer's case haunted me throughout my undergraduate years, and finally, when I reached graduate school, I began to find the means to respond to my need to know more—in rhetorical criticism. While historical, political, and legal analyses explained well the clashing forces that characterized the 1950s, no one explained just how the nation's most prestigious scientist was removed from public service. That is the focus of this book.

Larger issues inevitably emerge from a rhetorical analysis such as this one. My research on Oppenheimer's role, in nuclear development in particular, led to broader consideration of the interactions between the scientific and political worlds. What eventually intrigued me the most was the way the isolated, highly technical and mystical world of science and its Progress was interpreted in political terms for those of us on the Outside. The Oppenheimer case demonstrates clearly the merging of scientific and political terminologies and the influence that such a philosophical and rhetorical union can have on policy. Oppenheimer opposed the government's and nation's terminological orientation, both literally and figuratively, and, as a result, was removed from government service. The chapters that follow explain the rhetorical strategies the government used in making its case against Oppenheimer and suggest how Oppenheimer might have fought back more effectively.

Many people have encouraged and influenced my thinking about this area of inquiry. I owe thanks to professors Barry Brummett, Richard E. Crable, Charles J. Stewart, and especially Steven L. Vibbert, for their example as teachers and scholars. A host of colleagues and friends at Purdue University also endured and responded to endless discussions about "those scientists." A heartfelt thank-you is extended to Denise M. Bostdorff, Daniel O'Rourke, and Jennifer Stone, who listened beyond reasonable expectation.

My colleagues in the Department of Communication Studies at Virginia Polytechnic Institute and State University also deserve a word of appreciation. They have given me the moral and intellectual support I need to continue my growth as a scholar. A special thanks goes to my department head, Robert E. Denton. His ability to provide the institutional support necessary to a young faculty in very difficult economic times amazes me. But even more importantly, despite increasing administrative duties, he continues to lead by example, both in his teaching and scholarship. I am honored to be his colleague and his friend.

Finally, thanks to my family, who continue to believe in everything I do even when they are not exactly sure what that is.

NOTE

1. Berke Breathed. "Bloom County," *Washington Post*, 23 March 1985, F24.

Chapter 1

Introduction

> There is a dramatic moment and the history of the man, what made him
> act, what he did, and what sort of person he was. That is what you are
> really doing here. You are writing a man's life.
>
> Isidor I. Rabi,
> 1954 Security Hearing

Readers who opened the 29 March 1954 issue of *Life* magazine saw a shock-
ing and unprecedented series of photographs. Four pages described a
hydrogen bomb test gone wrong. A Japanese fishing boat had wandered too
near the explosion, and the result was devastating. The entire crew suffered
from radiation poisoning. The ship's cargo of fish was impounded and then
destroyed. Citizens of the United States, and the world, began to ask
questions.[1]

The Atomic Energy Commission (AEC) chairman, Lewis Strauss, responded to mounting public pressure for information in a news conference
a few days later. He reported that the hydrogen bomb could destroy an area
the size of the New York City metropolitan area. He also reinforced the
government's commitment to hydrogen bomb development, due to the
Soviet Union's demonstrated atomic bomb capability.[2]

The government released further reports about the nation's hydrogen
bomb program. *Life* shared the information on 12 April 1954. Time-lapse
photography of the hydrogen bomb's mushroom cloud fit easily among the
advertisements for new and improved luxury automobiles, refrigerators,

electric razors, air conditioners, and other wonders of modern technology.[3] Another article celebrated the University of California's new bevatron, which was opening new avenues of research into the mystery of the atom. Not unlike a commercial, the headline read, "New and Mightier Atom Smasher."[4] With *Life*'s next issue, the hydrogen bomb moved to new heights in our awareness. The magazine's cover and four pages within showed the first color photographs of the world's newest and most awesome destructive force.[5] Although the weapon inspired fear, Americans implicitly were reassured that the United States alone had the Nuclear Age's most powerful weapon . . . for now.

The next week's *Life* magazine revealed yet another side of America's scientific progress. After thumbing past the many advertisements, the readers came upon an unusual photograph. Instead of the typical close-ups of smiling celebrities, the subjects in the photograph were distant. Five men walked soberly through a parking lot toward the camera. Their faces were unclear. A badge and uniform identified one as a security officer, and three others were dressed in nondescript suits. The group's final member was easy to recognize, however, despite the distance. Walking out in front, tall and thin, wearing his trademark porkpie hat, J. Robert Oppenheimer, father of the atomic bomb, was the reason for the photographer's interest. The nation's most prestigious scientist was under investigation. The accompanying text reported that the AEC had raised questions about whether Oppenheimer's continued employment posed a security risk to the nation. The charges against Oppenheimer recounted old concerns about past communist associations and added another: "that Oppenheimer had opposed and then deliberately hindered U.S. development of the H-bomb."[6]

The investigation of Oppenheimer's life shocked the nation. Only a few years earlier, *Life* had devoted entire pages to Oppenheimer's strikingly angular face in a close-up feature story. He had appeared on the cover of *Time* twice, was the focus of stories in the *New York Times Magazine* and *Reader's Digest*, and was lauded as a hero among American scientists. From 1945 until 1954, few scientists had enjoyed greater public acclaim than Oppenheimer. After World War II, Oppenheimer had become known as the "father of the atomic bomb," due to his successful wartime supervision of the Los Alamos laboratory, the secret complex where U.S. scientists built the first atomic bomb. He had then become a respected government advisor on both technical and policy matters. As Herbert York, a fellow Los Alamos scientist, noted of Oppenheimer:

the remarkable web of interconnected advisory posts, in combination with his great intellectual power and the special mystique which surrounded him as a result of his having directed the central part of the atomic bomb program, made him by far the most influential nuclear scientist in America during the immediate postwar period.[7]

Then, in late 1953, everything changed for Oppenheimer. On 7 November, William Liscum Borden, former executive director of the Joint Congressional Committee on Atomic Energy, sent a letter to J. Edgar Hoover in which he accused Oppenheimer of espionage. Borden's evidence was not new. Throughout the 1930s and early 1940s, Oppenheimer had associated with known Communists. Although security officials expressed concern about Oppenheimer's associations, he received high-level security clearance in both 1943 and 1947, due initially to a belief that he was indispensable to the atomic bomb project. Later, after Oppenheimer's success at Los Alamos, his prestige and the insight he could provide to government as a leader in the American scientific community silenced critics.

But much changed between 1945 and 1954. The Soviet Union quickly transformed from an ally into a new and powerful enemy. The Iron Curtain divided the world. At home, Sen. Joseph McCarthy stirred American fear and hatred of Communists. Within government circles, Oppenheimer's ongoing criticism of U.S. military policy angered high-ranking officials in the military and Congress. The Strategic Air Command, in particular, found Oppenheimer's influence a barrier to its goals. Political appointments worked against Oppenheimer as well. The newly appointed chairman of the AEC, Lewis Strauss, was a long-time critic and opponent of Oppenheimer. The Republican members of the Joint Congressional Committee on Atomic Energy disliked Oppenheimer's advice. Thus, when Borden accused Oppenheimer of serving Soviet interests as a spy, many high-ranking and influential officials supported an investigation.

On 2 December 1953, President Eisenhower ordered a "blank wall" against Oppenheimer and thereby suspended the security clearance necessary to his advisory role. The AEC launched a full-scale investigation of Oppenheimer's past. As a result of the investigation, on 21 December the AEC general manager, Maj. Gen. Kenneth D. Nichols, sent a letter to Oppenheimer in which he raised questions about Oppenheimer's veracity, conduct and loyalty. Oppenheimer replied on 4 March 1953 with a letter that requested an official hearing and answered Nichols's charges. The Personnel Security Board listened to testimony throughout April 1954, and then deemed Oppenheimer's continued employment a risk to the national security. Oppenheimer appealed the decision to the AEC. On 29 June 1954, one day before Oppenheimer's consulting contract would have ended, the AEC officially removed Oppenheimer's security clearance. Oppenheimer never again served his government.

The response to Oppenheimer's removal was dramatic. The Federation of American Scientists admonished the government: "Seldom on this side of the Iron Curtain has a citizen who has served his country as well as Robert Oppenheimer been more miserably rewarded by his Government."[8] Albert Einstein wrote, "The systematic and widespread attempt to destroy mutual trust and confidence constitutes the severest possible blow against society."[9] The *Washington Post* raised "haunting questions":

In light of the exhaustive scrutiny of his [Oppenheimer's] personal life to which Dr. Oppenheimer has been subjected, can anyone with originality and ideas fully satisfy the standards of character and associations which the AEC has prescribed? And most important and most profound of all, will the security of the country really be stronger because Dr. Oppenheimer has been excluded from the program to which he has contributed so much?[10]

Years later, in 1982, a *Newsweek* writer described Oppenheimer's case as "at once a spellbinding scientific detective story, an upper-crust soap opera, an espionage thriller, a political chiller and a morality play with no clear cut sinners."[11] To this day, the case remains intriguing and dramatic.

OPPENHEIMER'S CASE REVISITED

The Oppenheimer question attracted, and continues to attract, scholars from a range of fields. Peter Goodchild, Denise Royal, Peter Michelmore, James W. Kunetka, and others attempt to capture Oppenheimer's complex personality for their readers.[12] York and Nuel Pharr Davis explore Oppenheimer's role in nuclear weapons development.[13] Still others emphasize the implications of Oppenheimer's case for science and politics. Donald W. Cox writes, "The trial bitterly accentuated the political breach within the scientific community and marked the end of the period of political innocence for the scientists."[14] Other analysts explain that much of the controversy that surrounded the case developed "over the entire record of relations between government and scientists, over the operation of the 'security system,' and over the development of national military policy."[15] Joseph Haberer discusses the Oppenheimer case extensively in his work *Politics and the Community of Science*, explaining that "it illustrates the dynamic relations of scientists to government with extraordinary clarity."[16] Haberer suggests that the 1954 security hearing was brought about by competition among scientific, military, political, and administrative coalitions, and he identifies as pivotal to the hearing's initiation the shift in AEC administration, the Army's weak position at the time, and the Soviet detonation of a thermonuclear device.

A similar concern for political motive is shown in Ralph E. Lapp's commentary on the Oppenheimer Case in *The New Priesthood: The Scientific Elite and the Uses of Power*. Believing that the case "was a direct result of intercult feuding," Lapp argues that Oppenheimer simply wrote the wrong report at the wrong time.

The Pentagon, particularly the Air Force, was notoriously intolerant of "outsiders" interfering with its strategic policy determinations. Oppenheimer's mistake was to author certain sections of a report (Project Vista) which challenged the strategic doctrine of the U.S. Air Force.[17]

Whether or not the case arose from political motives, as Lapp seems to suggest, or merely from a unique constellation of forces, it did crystallize a critical struggle between scientists and government.

The Oppenheimer case represents a watershed moment for security policy as well. Since the Oppenheimer hearing transcript was the first such document made available after the enactment of the 1947 AEC loyalty-security program and Eisenhower's 1953 federal employees security program, it gave legal theorists their first opportunity to examine carefully the U.S. security system. The hearing largely failed to meet the legal standards appropriate to such a government inquiry. In his scathing, book-length critique *The Oppenheimer Case: The Trial of a Security System*, Charles P. Curtis compares the Oppenheimer hearing to Joan of Arc's trial.[18] Harry Kalven, Jr., also a professor of law, reaches the similar, if more subtle, conclusion that the AEC made either "a most serious error of judgment in applying standards" or "implicit use of general security standards so stringent and puritanical as to give cause for alarm."[19] Both authors also note suspect procedure used by the Gray Board and the distinctly argumentative style of the Gray Board counsel, Roger Robb, as factors that made the hearing more of a trial, rather than the prescribed inquiry. Kalven concludes his criticism in Oppenheimer's favor. He writes, "As we noted at the start, the Gray Report recognized that the security system was on trial along with Dr. Oppenheimer. It is the security system and not Dr. Oppenheimer that, in the end, has lost its case."[20]

The work that synthesizes the biographical, political, and legal considerations of the case, and thus emerges as the seminal work on the Oppenheimer case, is Philip M. Stern's *The Oppenheimer Case: Security on Trial*. Stern gives the reader a sense of the man, the turbulence of the period, and the complexity of forces that led to the hearing. He then provides a painstaking analysis of the hearing itself and its results. Stern critiques the legality of the hearing, suggests its importance as a test case, and discusses the implications for those involved and for the country as a whole.[21]

What many authors only imply becomes the focus of *The Great Weapons Heresy*, by Thomas W. Wilson, Jr. Wilson asks, "Why did the United States government single out a particular advisor—in this case the most prestigious of its consultants—and, at a particular time, drive him from government service?"[22] Wilson concludes that Oppenheimer's call for the containment of nuclear arms development amounted to heresy in the dominant arms-buildup religion of the 1950s. Accordingly, Oppenheimer was excommunicated.

While Wilson's analysis is intriguing, he and others do not address the importance of the hearing's rhetoric as the means to justify Oppenheimer's removal. Whatever the motives behind Oppenheimer's removal, the process through which that removal was accomplished holds significant implications for the political process. Thus, I propose a shift in emphasis that makes rhetoric, not personality conflicts or political forces or procedural concerns, the central analytic focus. This book answers the questions, How did the U.S. government single out a particular advisor—in this case, the most prestigious of its consultants—and, at a particular time, drive him from government service? and How did the government legitimize that decision for the American public? The rhetoric of Oppenheimer's security hearing essentially rewrote his life, and as such offers a unique opportunity to explore the broader issue of transformation of political persona.

Our terminologies, suggests Kenneth Burke, define and express "how things were, how things are and how they may be."[23] Rhetoric helps to guide decision making; rhetoric forms frames of acceptance, which are "the more or less organized system(s) of meanings by which a thinking man gauges the historical situation and adopts a role with relation to it."[24] Ray E. McKerrow notes that

the rhetoric of our past conditions and constrains the strategic choices we make in the present. This "truism" assumes that rhetoric defines an individual's perceptions of the social reality in which he moves, decides, and ultimately acts.[25]

Our frames of acceptance allow present and future interpretations in terms of previously identified patterns of experience. They also may promote reevaluation of past events in terms of new and different names that simplify and interpret reality. Quite often, history is rewritten based on reinterpretations, and sometimes individual personae are transformed in the process. The creation, maintenance, denigration, and transformation of public personae is central to U.S. politics and is clearly revealed in "the matter of J. Robert Oppenheimer." Oppenheimer's removal from government service, his rhetorical transformation from hero to villain, provides the rhetoric that this book explores.

POLITICS, RHETORIC, AND SELF-DEFENSE

Stories of challenged character intrigue Americans. Whether the tale involves Richard Nixon's proud defense of Checkers and Pat's cloth coat, Jimmy Swaggert's tearful pleas for forgiveness of sin, or Pete Rose's reluctant admission that his actions may have damaged the institution of baseball, Americans are drawn to the drama that calls forth apologia, speeches of self-defense. Edward P. J. Corbett notes that we may enjoy this human spectacle because secretly we say to ourselves, "Ah, there but for the grace of God go I."[26] At another level, these cases expose our fundamental beliefs about what it means to be human. Are our acts indicative of our character, or are we created through our acts? Are we the products of our environment, or are we as human beings uniquely capable of controlling our world? Where does responsibility reside?

Kenneth Burke notes that five key terms encompass the range of human interpretations of situations and attributions of motives: act, scene, agent, purpose, and agency.[27] When explanations of actions emphasize one term over another, differing expectations and evaluations of actions result. For instance, Barry Brummett's analysis of a gay rights controversy shows that an interpretation of human motivation that emphasizes acts results in completely different evaluations and policies than an interpretation that focuses on agents. Pro-gay rights arguments emphasize "gayness" as a condition of being, as central to the agent's identity, just as "blackness" or "Jewishness" would be. Pro-gay rights advocates stress that the agent's right to *be* gay is separate from approval of his/her acts. The resultant political action is protection of gay rights due to their defined minority status.

Anti-gay rights arguments flip the equation, assuming, Brummett explains, that "a person is gay because he/she *does* something."[28] Gayness is an act—a life-style or behavior. As a result, anti-gay rights advocates argue that gay individuals choose to act gay and thus should be held responsible for what anti-gay rights groups consider immoral acts. Gay people should cease their "gay acts" or be punished accordingly.

Still others argue that gay-ness results from something within a young person's "scene"—family conditions or childhood trauma. If something external to the agent causes gayness and the goal is to eliminate gay behaviors, then the appropriate response is to change the scene. Gay individuals cannot reasonably be blamed for their behaviors if the behaviors result from uncontrollable external forces.

Brummett's analysis highlights the symbolic nature of political controversy. The facts that surround gay rights are the same for both the pro- and the anti- forces. What changes is the orientation that different people use to interpret those facts. Their political responses to the issue are consistent with, and indeed grow out of, their orientations. Not only do both orientations consider what it means to be sexual or political, but as Brummett so keenly points out, the orientations define what it means to be human. At some level, all analyses of apologia address that fundamental issue. Because interpretations of human action reside in the world of words, people may use words to defend and transform negative evaluations of their characters. The same interpretations that generate evaluation and accusation likewise provide potential defense.

In the past thirty years, rhetorical critics have established the classical genre of an apologia, or speech of self-defense, perhaps more completely than any other form of public address. From characteristics generated through case study analysis of individual speeches and comparisons of mul-

tiple apologetic speeches, scholars have come to general agreement on
several defining characteristics of apologia. The first is that an apologia
responds to questions raised about a person's "moral nature, motives, and
reputation."[29] Rhetorical scholars differentiate a defense of character from
a defense of policy. B. L. Ware and Wil Linkugel assert that "the question-
ing of a man's moral nature, motives, or reputation is qualitatively different
from the challenging of his policies."[30] However, as Halford Ross Ryan
notes, a rhetor's acts or policies may be central to a defense of character. A
forced separation of policy and character limits a critic's ability to explore
strategies of apologia. Indeed, in some cases, policy and character are
inseparable.[31]

A second understood, if not always stated, characteristic of apologia is
the necessity of some kind of exigence; apologia is offered in response to
some accusation. Noreen Wales Kruse incorporated these essential characteristics in this definition of apologia: "public discourse produced whenever
a prominent person attempts to repair his character if it has been directly or
indirectly damaged by overt charges, or rumors and allegations, which
negatively value his behavior and/or his judgments."[32] An apologia is, by
definition, a response to a challenge to ethos or character.

Kruse gave the first explicit attention to a third element of the apologetic
genre, the ethical context. She highlighted the primary importance of standards of judgment to apologetic rhetoric. Neither accusations nor defense
can be offered or analyzed apart from the ethics that determine what is
good and bad. Kruse demonstrated the role of ethical standards in her
insightful examination of self-defense in team sports.

Kruse identified a unique set of values that guide the world of team sport.
Ethical athletes must be the best they can possibly be; must place team
interests above individual interests; must display devotion to the team, the
game, and the world of sport; and must never concede defeat until the game
is complete. Accusations arise and a self-defense is offered only when
athletes appear to violate these values. Kruse notes that "sports personalities must defend their worth *as sports figures* whenever their conduct might
have harmful effects upon teams, games, or the world of sport."[33]
Moreover, some actions might violate a broader social ethic but not require
apologia within the world of sports. For instance, when James Worthy, a
professional basketball star, failed to play in the first half of a game because
he was under arrest for soliciting a prostitute, the accusation against him in
the world of sports was not that he had violated law and accepted moral
standards, but that he had placed personal interests ahead of team interests.
Fortunately for his team, he arrived in time to score twenty-five points in
the game's second half and secured a win. Thus his actions redeemed his
earlier failure. This case and Kruse's discussion demonstrate clearly that
every accusation and every apologia reflects a set of evaluative standards.[34]

While most scholars past and present would accept these defining qualities of apologia, some notable disagreements in apologia studies involve the critical task itself. Kruse challenged the "single speech" approach traditionally used to study apologia. She argued that if the rhetorical context (the need for an accusation) is a "requisite for determining what does and does not constitute apologia, we can assume that the veracity of the need for an apologetic response is more significant than the medium in which it is presented."[35] For Kruse, apologia could be presented in a play, a novel, or even a cartoon. Perhaps the simplest definition of apologia comes from her argument that "apologia is a specific mode of discourse which is generated in response to an exigence."[36] Apologia is not, by definition, a single speech. Studies by D. Ray Heisey, George N. Dionisopoulos, Steven L. Vibbert, and others reinforce Kruse's contention.[37]

The necessity of an exigence, some charge against a person's character, also prompted Ryan's criticism and extension of apologia studies. Ryan rightly points to a lack of attention paid to the accusation in contemporary rhetorical criticism. Although critics had established and discussed the exigence prior to Ryan's critique, and Kruse had explicitly identified rhetorical context as a key definitional demand, Ryan's complaint focused on the type of attention given the accusation. He argued that the accusation, or kategoria, exhibits generic affinities just as important and identifiable as the apologia's and should be studied as a mode of discourse, not just as the catalyst for apologia. To fill the void, he suggested that the accusation and defense be studied as a speech set. He argued that "by checking each speech against the other, the critic is better able to distinguish the vital issues from the spurious ones, to evaluate the relative merits of both speakers' arguments, and to make an assessment of the relative failure or success of both speakers in terms of the final outcome of the speech set."[38] Not only has Ryan demonstrated the value of such a critical method, but an entire volume of critical works explores kategoria and apologia as interdependent discourses.[39]

This book takes Ryan's admonition—that the accusation and the defense must be treated as separate and interrelated modes of discourse that can be best understood through comparison—and then goes one step further and links the accusation and defense to the official documents that form the decision in the case. Just as analysis of the accusation sheds light on the apologetic response, decisional statements reveal the strengths and weaknesses in the earlier discourse. Likewise, the decisional statements, as discourse, can be understood better when compared to the earlier stages of the apologetic process. This extension of the apologetic process to include decisional statements is an attempt to increase the information available to the critic and thereby to improve the critic's interpretation and evaluation of rhetorical strategies.

This book offers a final extension to studies of apologia and rhetorical criticism generally. In order to fully understand and interpret the strategies employed by rhetors, a critic must follow a systematic method that both incorporates the influence of the broad evaluative frame created in social and political interaction and attends to the specific terminological choices that rhetors make. Often, methods deal with one aspect at the expense of another. The broad social frame is not fully integrated with the microscopic terminological analysis, or specific rhetorical characteristics of the discourse are lost in the analysis of the broader rhetorical objectives. The method outlined in Chapter 3, called terminological algebra, provides critics with a flexible approach to microscopic analysis that incorporates the evaluative context so central to apologia.

When terminological choice comprises the critical focus, as it does in this book, virtually any case of rhetoric can be studied. The Oppenheimer case rhetoric, however, exhibits several striking terminological features that make its examination especially profitable. First, terms such as "loyalty," "veracity," and "character" were used both to support and to degrade Oppenheimer's security position. Opposing rhetors generally do not build their cases upon the same pivotal terms. The Oppenheimer case, therefore, furnishes a unique example of terminological interaction of terms in opposed discourse.

Second, the public documents of the case "name" events gathered into a then well-known body of evidence. A detailed account of Oppenheimer's life had been prepared for the Gray Board, primarily from the FBI's eleven-year continuous surveillance of Oppenheimer and his family. The "facts" of the case had been known for some time. Twice, in 1943 and 1947, Oppenheimer had received security clearance based on this information. Nevertheless, in 1954 the very same evidence led to his dismissal. Although many scholars and others offer political explanations for the government's reversal, the public documents suggest a rhetorical explanation. As was suggested earlier, Oppenheimer's life was "rewritten." Hearing testimony and decision documents assigned new evaluations to his past acts, and as a result, he lost his security clearance. In addition to a political process, a rhetorical process was operating. The case, therefore, may yield insights into the use of evidence as an evolving and dynamic persuasive resource.

Third, Oppenheimer's case demonstrates the importance of context. Words mean different things at different times. Key terms in the case, such as "communist" and "loyalty," had shifted dramatically during Oppenheimer's tenure in government service. That shift is central to the case and to a rhetorical explanation of the political decision.

Fourth, the public documents of the Oppenheimer case reflect strategic choices made by opposing rhetors. Oppenheimer answered Nichols's letter of charges with his own statement of self-defense. The Personnel Security

Board reviewed both the charges and the defense, as well as weeks of testimony. The majority decisions of the Gray Board and the AEC upheld the import of Nichols's accusations and recommended that Oppenheimer lose his security clearance. Examination of these documents reveals noteworthy strategies used by opposed rhetors.

Finally, and most significantly, the Oppenheimer case exemplifies the kind of difficult determination encountered by anyone who participates in U.S. politics. While Oppenheimer's past was explicitly at issue, the ultimate decision to be made was about his future. Was his continued employment a risk to national security? The judges had to predict Oppenheimer's future behavior. Americans make a similar decision when they elect officials. The voters listen to the candidates, consider their present and past actions, and observe them in an attempt to decide which they will trust to serve their interests and the interests of the country. As long as "character" factors into that decision, and as long as words frame our political reality, cases of political apologia warrant attention. According to Aristotle, the study of rhetoric promotes a critical citizenry. My hope is that this book may contribute to that effort.

NOTES

1. Dwight Martin, "First Casualties of the H-Bomb," *Life*, 29 March 1954, 17-21.

2. William L. Laurence, "Vast Power Bared: March 1 Explosion Was Equivalent to Millions of Tons of TNT," *New York Times*, 1 April 1954, A1.

3. "5-4-3-2-1 and the Hydrogen Age Is upon Us," *Life*, 12 April 1954, 24-32.

4. "New and Mightier Atom Smasher," *Life*, 12 April 1954, 62-66.

5. "Color Photographs Add Vivid Reality to Nation's Concept of H-Bomb," *Life*, 19 April 1954, 21-24.

6. "U.S. Ponders a Scientist's Past," *Life*, 26 April 1954, 35.

7. Herbert York, *The Advisors: Oppenheimer, Teller, and the Superbomb* (San Francisco: W. H. Freeman, 1976), 20.

8. "Scientists Are Disappointed," *New York Times*, 30 June 1954, A10.

9. "Scientists Affirm Faith in Oppenheimer," *Bulletin of the Atomic Scientists* 10 (1954): 190.

10. Editorial, "Security Risk," *Washington Post*, 1 July 1954, 14.

11. "The Man Who Made the Bomb," *Newsweek*, 10 May 1982, 65.

12. See Peter Goodchild, *J. Robert Oppenheimer: Shatterer of Worlds* (Boston: Houghton Mifflin, 1981); Denise Royal, *The Story of J. Robert Oppenheimer* (New York: St Martin's, 1969); Peter Michelmore, *The Swift Years: The Robert Oppenheimer Story* (New York: Dodd, Mead, 1969); James W. Kunetka, *Oppenheimer: The Years of Risk* (Englewood Cliffs, N.J.: Prentice-Hall, 1982).

13. See York, *Advisors*; and Nuel Pharr Davis, *Lawrence and Oppenheimer*, reprint of 1968 edition (New York: Da Capo, 1986).

14. Donald W. Cox, *America's New Policy Makers: The Scientists' Rise to Power* (New York: Chilton, 1964), 39.

15. J. Stephan Dupré and Sanford A. Lakoff, *Science and the Nation: Policy and Politics* (Englewood Cliffs, N.J.: Prentice-Hall, 1962), 142.

16. Joseph Haberer, *Politics and the Community of Science* (New York: Van Nostrand Reinhold, 1969), 217.

17. Ralph E. Lapp, *The New Priesthood: The Scientific Elite and the Uses of Power* (New York: Harper and Row, 1965), 108.

18. Charles P. Curtis, *The Oppenheimer Case: Trial of a Security System* (New York: Simon and Schuster, 1955).

19. Harry Kalven, Jr., "The Case of J. Robert Oppenheimer before the Atomic Energy Commission," *Bulletin of the Atomic Scientists* 10 (1954): 259.

20. Ibid., 269.

21. Philip M. Stern, *The Oppenheimer Case: Security on Trial* (New York: Harper and Row, 1969).

22. Thomas W. Wilson, Jr., *The Great Weapons Heresy* (Boston: Houghton Mifflin, 1970), xviii.

23. Kenneth Burke, *Permanence and Change: An Anatomy of Purpose*, 3rd ed. (Berkeley: University of California Press, 1984), 14. Burke suggests in a later passage that a person's explanation of attitudes and motives involves the statement of that person's orientation or general view of the world. See p. 20.

24. Kenneth Burke, *Attitudes toward History*, 3d ed. (Berkeley: University of California Press, 1984), 5.

25. Ray E. McKerrow, "Truman and Korea: Rhetoric in the Pursuit of Victory," *Central States Speech Journal* 28 (1977): 1.

26. Edward P. J. Corbett, Foreword to Halford Ross Ryan, ed., *Oratorical Encounters: Selected Studies and Sources of Twentieth-Century Political Accusations and Apologies* (New York: Greenwood, 1988), xi.

27. Kenneth Burke, *A Grammar of Motives*, reprint of 1945 edition (Berkeley: University of California Press, 1969), xv.

28. Barry Brummett, "A Pentadic Analysis of Ideologies in Two Gay Rights Controversies," *Central States Speech Journal* 30 (1979): 255.

29. B. L. Ware and Wil Linkugel, "They Spoke in Defense of Themselves: On the Generic Criticism of Apologia," *Quarterly Journal of Speech* 59 (1973): 273-83.

30. Ibid., 274.

31. See Halford Ross Ryan, introduction to Ryan, ed., *Oratorical Encounters*, xxii-xxiii.

32. Noreen Wales Kruse, "Motivational Factors in Non-Denial Apologia," *Central States Speech Journal* 28 (1977): 13.

33. Noreen Wales Kruse, "Apologia in Team Sport," *Quarterly Journal of Speech* 67 (1981): 274.

34. Richard E. Crable also explores the role of ethical standards in questions of accountability and proposes nine different argumentative strategies that rhetors might use in responding to accusations. See Richard E. Crable, "Ethical Codes, Accountability, and Argumentation," *Quarterly Journal of Speech* 64 (1978): 23-32.

35. Noreen Wales Kruse, "The Scope of Apologetic Discourse: Establishing Generic Parameters," *Southern Speech Communication Journal* 46 (1981): 282.

36. Ibid., 291.

37. D. Ray Heisey, "President Ronald Reagan's Apologia on the Iran-Contra Affair," in Ryan, ed., *Oratorical Encounters*, 281-305; George N. Dionisopoulos and Steven L. Vibbert, "CBS vs. Mobil Oil: Charges of Creative Bookkeeping in 1979," in Ryan, ed., *Oratorical Encounters*, 241-52.

38. Halford Ross Ryan, "Kategoria and Apologia: On Their Rhetorical Criticism as a Speech Set," *Quarterly Journal of Speech* 68 (1982): 254.

39. See Ryan, ed., *Oratorical Encounters*.

Chapter 2

Oppenheimer's Rise to Power:
The Historical Prelude

By 1954, J. Robert Oppenheimer had developed a reputation, as Stern notes, for

a superlatively quick mind; a supreme command of the word; an almost hypnotic power to captivate, inspire, persuade, stimulate. Within this same human being, however, there lived an opposite force: a capacity to belittle, wither, antagonize, alienate.[1]

Oppenheimer's positive qualities had led him to a distinguished career in academia and government service, but at the same time, his negative qualities had engendered animosity. Few people who knew and worked with Oppenheimer reported ambivalence in their feelings about him. His supporters were unfailingly loyal. As the 1954 hearing began, the atomic energy commissioner, Sumner Pike, observed of the accusations lodged against Oppenheimer, "These things are so incredible to me that I almost wonder if there isn't some other motivation behind the apparent one in bringing these charges at this time."[2] A review of Oppenheimer's record both supports Pike's incredulity and exposes the roots of the "other motivation," which was equally part of Oppenheimer's past.

THE ACADEMIC YEARS: OPPENHEIMER FINDS HIS POLITICAL IDENTITY

During his early career, Oppenheimer was immersed in the life of an intellectual. He earned his bachelor's degree from Harvard in 1925 and then his doctoral credentials from Göttingen two years later. He studied with Max Born and Paul Dirac and, through his extensions of their work, became known to physicists throughout Europe and the United States. Oppenheimer met his lifelong friend Isidor I. Rabi during this period. Rabi believed at the time, and never wavered from his belief, that Oppenheimer had the best mind of his generation. He predicted that Oppenheimer would make the United States an international center for theoretical physics.[3]

Oppenheimer returned to the United States and began to realize his dream in 1929, when he accepted concurrent appointments in theoretical physics at the California Institute of Technology and at the University of California, Berkeley. He joined the company of other American scientists, among them Charles Lauritsen and Ernest Lawrence. Theoretical physics in the United States was new and exciting, and Oppenheimer quickly became known as one of the nation's most skilled teachers. Nuel Pharr Davis reports that Oppenheimer "became recognized as the best native physics teacher of his time."[4]

During these years, Oppenheimer had little contact with, or interest in, politics. He exemplified academic eccentricity and lived quite untouched by practical concerns. Born to a wealthy family, Oppenheimer lived quite apart from the world, insulated not only from the career pressures that motivated his peers, but also from the political, social, and economic issues of the day. He later admitted that he had learned of the 1929 stock market crash only well after the event.

In 1936, however, Oppenheimer experienced a political awakening. As he watched his students struggle against the impact of the Depression and empathized with German relatives oppressed by antisemitism, Oppenheimer was moved to participate in and contribute to political causes, many of them closely linked to the Communist party. At the time, sympathy with communist causes was common among socially conscious intellectuals. The fact that Oppenheimer never officially joined the Communist party suggests that his particular group of friends, perhaps more than communist doctrine, influenced his earliest political activities. His brother, sister-in-law, a former fiancée, his wife, and many friends were all, at one time, Communist party members. Many of Oppenheimer's students openly supported left-wing organizations. However loose his affiliation, these "communist associations" would provide much of the discrediting evidence presented at his security hearing some eighteen years later.

Oppenheimer's communist associations were short-lived, however. Working with three Soviet physicists, briefly in the mid-1930s, shifted his thinking again. Their description of life in a totalitarian state convinced Oppenheimer that his earlier views had been misguided and naive; his reading of Marx, Engels, and Lenin had not prepared him for the less than ideal conditions confronted by his colleagues as citizens of a communist state. This realization, furthered by several Soviet policy decisions, prompted Oppenheimer's disengagement from communist circles.

At the same time that Oppenheimer changed his political views, like many scientists, he began to express an interest in the potential power of the atom. Einstein's revolutionary thought made it theoretically possible to harness the atom's power. Atomic energy emerged as a new scientific frontier, in both Europe and the United States.

A second destructive force emerged in Europe around the same time— Hitler and the Third Reich. Hitler's force was demonstrated by 1939, when the atom's power was yet unrealized. U.S. scientists feared that Hitler might uncover and capture the atom's power. They reasoned that if U.S. physicists believed they could unlock and control the atom's explosive potential, the Germans also would recognize and pursue the possible military applications of atomic energy. Since scientists alone were aware of the atom's potential danger, several U.S. physicists felt it was their duty to alert the government.

Leo Szilard and Eugene Wigner persuaded Einstein to write a letter to President Franklin D. Roosevelt that explained atomic energy and its possible military uses. With the assistance of an economist, Alexander Sachs, who was one of President Roosevelt's personal advisors, the letter was brought to Roosevelt's attention and accomplished its purpose. The story goes that Roosevelt silently listened as Sachs argued for government-financed atomic research and then said, "Alex, what you are after is to see that the Nazis don't blow us up?"

Sachs replied, "Precisely."

Roosevelt then called in his attaché, General Edwin "Pa" Watson, pointed to Einstein's letter and other documents provided by the scientists, and said, "Pa, this requires action."[5]

Although not as swiftly as Szilard and others had hoped, action did come. After two preliminary research committees uncovered the problems scientists faced in atomic research, President Roosevelt created the Office for Scientific Research and Development (OSRD) on 28 June 1941. Under the direction of the Carnegie Institute's Vannevar Bush and his assistant, Karl T. Compton, a former president of the Massachusetts Institute of Technology, the OSRD supervised all scientific research, including the work in atomic fission.

Fission research, the most crucial to atomic weaponry, advanced dramatically in 1940-1941. At Berkeley, Lawrence and Glenn Seaborg made major discoveries about uranium and plutonium, the materials required for an atomic explosion. At almost the same time, the British reported that an atomic bomb could be developed in less than two years. Upon Bush's request, Roosevelt provided increased financial support for atomic weapons construction.

Although Oppenheimer had worked unofficially on Lawrence's research team, his first official connection with the growing secret research effort came in October 1941, when he became a member of a special committee that reviewed existing fission research. Also, in July 1942, Oppenheimer directed a small group that discussed yet another facet of fission research: atomic bomb design. Oppenheimer realized during this seminar that unless the many large, diverse laboratories needed to develop an atom bomb were centralized, the project might never succeed. The Nazi threat made unacceptable the slow progress typical of a scientific laboratory.

Oppenheimer's suggestion came at exactly the right time. Although the OSRD had advanced atomic research quickly, as the war continued, even greater security and speed were needed to develop feasible weapons. Hitler's threat still loomed, especially for Great Britain. In August 1942, Churchill and Roosevelt centered all Allied atomic research in Canada and the United States. At the same time, control over the project transferred from civilian to military agencies. The effort was named the Manhattan Project and was directed by Gen. Leslie Groves, Gen. Wilhelm D. Styer, and Adm. W.R.E. Purnell, with the assistance of Bush and James Conant. General Groves headed military applications and immediately approved Oppenheimer's recommendation to build the isolated, high-security weapons laboratory complex near Los Alamos, New Mexico. Groves appointed Oppenheimer as the laboratory director in early 1943. At the time, Army intelligence officers expressed concern over Oppenheimer's employment, due to his past communist associations. General Groves, however, felt that Oppenheimer was indispensable to the project and therefore personally requested Oppenheimer's security clearance. It was granted for the first time in December 1943.

THE LOS ALAMOS YEARS: OPPENHEIMER "FATHERS" THE ATOMIC BOMB

During his service as the Los Alamos laboratory director, Oppenheimer's leadership skills faced their most stringent test and his reputation soared as a result of his success. Joseph Haberer notes that Oppenheimer's time "was principally occupied with administrative problems, such as acquiring needed personnel, maintaining a workable balance between the miltary and the scientists, and resolving scientific and technical problems."[6] Oppenheimer's ability to persuade scientists to join the Los Alamos effort was critical to the project's success.

The project also required Oppenheimer to play an unusual role for a scientist. Scientific work operates through extensive peer review and revision. In some senses, all science is collaborative, and as such requires significant time to build consensus within a research area. At Los Alamos, however, the military constantly pushed for the earliest possible delivery of an atomic weapon. Hans Bethe noted that, although the war created pressure unusual for a scientific directorship, Oppenheimer handled the deadline well:

The most important, perhaps, were the decisions on which several possible methods for assembling an atomic bomb should be selected. . . . It is very easy to run a scientific development laboratory by pursuing all ideas which do not seem completely absurd. This keeps all scientists happy who propose ideas. . . . But in wartime we could not afford such luxury. . . . Oppenheimer was equal to the task. He made the correct technical decisions and even in retrospect, one can see that he made them in optimum time.[7]

Most observers agree about Oppenheimer's administrative excellence. Perhaps more interesting, however, are accounts that praise his managerial ability. Victor Weisskopf, a renowned scientist and a member of the Los Alamos team, described Oppenheimer's charismatic leadership in this way:

It was most impressive to see Oppie handle that mixture of international scientific prima donnas, engineers, and army officers. He forged them into an enthusiastically productive crowd. . . . His uncanny speed in grasping the main point of any subject was a decisive factor; he could acquaint himself with the essential details of every part of the work. He did not direct from the head office. He was intellectually and even physically present at each decisive step. . . . It wasn't that he contributed so many ideas or suggestions; he did sometimes but his main influence came from something else. It was his continuous and intense presence which produced a sense of direct participation in all of us; it created that unique atmosphere and challenge that prevailed in the place throughout its time.[8]

Whether it was due to the "unique atmosphere" or merely the concentration of scientific genius, the Los Alamos laboratory neared its objective— atom bomb production—early in 1945. In his first interview with President Truman, in April 1945, the secretary of war, Henry L. Stimson, urged Truman to create an expert committee to advise him on the possible use of the first atom bomb and on the future of the Manhattan Project. Truman took Stimson's advice and appointed an interim committee consisting of Stimson; his deputy, George L. Harrison; Truman's representative, James Byrnes; Ralph A. Bard of the Navy; William L. Clayton of the State Department; and scientists Bush, Conant, and Karl T. Compton. The committee was supported by an expert scientific panel made up of Oppenheimer, Enrico Fermi, Arthur H. Compton, and Lawrence. The interim committee's first challenge, as presented by Gen. George C. Marshall, was to consider "atomic energy not simply in terms of military weapons but also in terms of a new relationship of man and the universe."[9] The scientific panel received somewhat different orders.

Oppenheimer and Arthur C. Compton both believed that they had been asked to give a technical reply to a technical question—not whether the atom bomb should be used against Japan, but how.[10] Earlier that spring, Manhattan Project specialists had selected the sites in Japan most suitable as atomic bomb targets. From all reports, the military apparently never doubted that the bomb would be used.[11] Consequently, the scientific panel did not express the "no military use" position held by many atomic scientists. In defense of the scientific panel's recommendation to use the bomb, Oppenheimer said, "We thought the two overriding considerations were the saving of lives in the war and the effect of our actions . . . on our strength and the stability of the world. We did say that we did not think that exploding one of these things as a firecracker over a desert was likely to be very impressive."[12] Although the interim committee's recommendations were strictly secret, its findings quickly circulated throughout the project. Many scientists protested through secret channels. The atomic bomb decision thus marked the first major political division among scientists in the nuclear age.

While scientists, politicians, and military personnel discussed the bomb's use, the work at Los Alamos continued. The first atom bomb was tested at Alamagordo, New Mexico, on 16 July 1945. The size of the blast was even greater than expected. Immediately after the bomb exploded, Oppenheimer recalled a passage from a sacred Hindu epic:

> If the radiance of a thousand suns
> were to burst into the sky
> that would be like
> the splendor of the Mighty One.

A moment later, he thought of another line: "I am become Death, the shatterer of worlds." Oppenheimer captured the awe and sense of immense responsibility that many scientists felt. Fermi expressed the joy of scientific discovery. He said, "Don't bother me with your conscientious scruples. After all, the thing's superb physics."[13]

The bomb Little Boy was dropped on Hiroshima less than a month after the Alamagordo test. Although it may have been superb physics, the atomic bomb was no firecracker. Oppenheimer became known as the "father of the atomic bomb"; he was instrumental not only in its creation, but also in its introduction to the world.

Oppenheimer's success at Los Alamos earned him the U.S. Medal for Merit in 1946 and propelled him into further government service. Although he wished to return to teaching, Oppenheimer's knowledge of atomic weaponry and power, his ability to explain complex concepts to laypersons, and his "special Los Alamos mystique" made him an immediate choice, as the government began to grapple with the military and political ramifications of atomic energy.

THE ADVISORY YEARS: OPPENHEIMER FOLLOWS A CONTROVERSIAL "CONTROL" LINE

Oppenheimer's first advisory appointment was to the Acheson-Lilienthal Committee's scientific advisory board in January 1946. The committee's mandate was "to study the subject of controls and safeguards necessary to protect this Government.''[14] The committee was concerned primarily with international control of atomic energy. The members eventually proposed a solution similar to the U.S. Atomic Energy Act: the creation of an International Atomic Energy Development Agency. The agency would be a fully autonomous body that would regulate all distribution of fissionable materials and would supervise research and development of nondangerous uses for atomic energy. The agency would have the exclusive right to research atomic explosives. The committee's recommendations soon became the Baruch Plan, and were presented to the United Nations Atomic Energy Commission in 1946.

The Baruch Plan called for a radical step in atomic energy control. Despite the long-range peace interest central to the plan, the Soviet Union refused to subordinate its interests to an international agency and thus vetoed the plan. These events ended all hope of international control of nuclear energy. As Wilson notes, the early nuclear age was characterized by U.S. initiatives and responses to them.

The first major political act of the nuclear age was the U.S. decision to drop the bomb on Hiroshima and the second was the Japanese decision to surrender after Nagasaki; the third and fourth major political acts of the nuclear age were the U.S. decision to offer the Baruch Plan and the Soviet decision to reject it.[15]

Oppenheimer played a central role in both U.S. decisions. His presence at these critical moments added to the mystique already created at Los Alamos. Moreover, although he originally supported atom bomb use, Oppenheimer's association with the Baruch Plan helped to establish his image as a control advocate.

U.S. policy with regard to nuclear weapons was unclear immediately after World War II; later events complicated the issues further. Many scientists and politicians continued to second-guess the atomic bombing of the Japanese cities. The Baruch Plan failed in the United Nations. Scientists and others felt torn between the need to strengthen the country's defense and the need to make the future safe from nuclear holocaust. A rampant fear of communist takeover heightened emotions. The Cold War years of the Truman and Eisenhower administrations marked the beginning of a full-scale nuclear arms race. By the early 1950s, many Americans believed that successful development of the hydrogen bomb was essential to preserve the U.S. position as leader of the free world. Without the hydrogen bomb, the United States could not triumph in the international struggle for military superiority.

Others, with Oppenheimer a key advocate among them, favored limited nuclear development, and therefore a controversy arose over hydrogen bomb development within the scientific community and beyond. Robert Gilpin divides the scientists into two schools of thought: the finite containment school and the infinite containment school.

The finite containment school, led by Oppenheimer, hoped to limit the nuclear arms race "by international agreement at some finite point prior to the settlement of political differences between the United States and the Soviet Union while at the same time it is also necessary to contain Soviet aggression."[16] These scientists argued that their duty was to "assist mankind to keep political developments abreast of technical advancement."[17] Hydrogen bomb development, to them, seemed premature. The infinite containment school, led primarily by Edward Teller, held that international agreement was impossible in the foreseeable future and that the nuclear arms race must continue. The United States would maintain its leadership, in this view, only by developing the hydrogen bomb as soon as possible.[18] Oppenheimer expressed this philosophy in a third important policy recommendation—the decision that may have contributed the most to his 1954 problems.

In October 1949, the general advisory committee to the AEC was asked to make a recommendation about hydrogen bomb development. The committee concluded that the hydrogen bomb did not warrant the funding necessary for a crash development program, partly due to technical infeasibility, but also on moral grounds. Oppenheimer, as chairman of the committee, became the spokesperson for the recommendation.

Richard T. Sylves argues that the meetings on the superbomb were one of the committee's greatest tests. Political, moral, and ethical questions were intertwined with technical considerations. The scientists reasoned that the superbomb should not be developed because it "appeared to be both expensive and difficult to make, because it would undercut new fission bomb work in progress, because it had a yet undetermined military utility, and because its destructive power would be catastrophically immense."[19] They argued that the United States could gain "considerable moral prestige at very little cost" if it renounced the superbomb. These scientists' recommendations, Sylves asserts, "stand as evidence that scientists and engineers engaged in defense-related research can appreciate and anticipate the moral and ethical implications surrounding the products of their research."[20]

The matter, as policy, ended on 31 January 1950, when President Truman gave the go-ahead on hydrogen bomb research. However noble the position of the AEC general advisory committee, political and military leaders disagreed strenuously with its recommendation. The "hydrogen bomb question" created a rift among U.S. scientists, and also a rift between science and politics. The controversy was so great, argue both York and Sylves, that Oppenheimer's security hearing was a direct result of his participation in the committee's ruling.[21]

Oppenheimer's depth of involvement in government consulting, as well as his frequent public speaking engagements, made him perhaps the most visible and influential scientist in the United States in the late 1940s and early 1950s. Besides his appearance on a *Time* cover in November 1948,

Oppenheimer's "look"—tall, gaunt, a cigarette and a porkpie hat—was so well known that the first cover of *Physics Today*, which featured a porkpie hat resting on industrial plumbing, was immediately understood as a tribute to Oppenheimer. His status was high in both scientific and public circles. The restrained "nuclear control" path he followed, however, led him increasingly into unpopular and controversial territory.

Many analysts believe that because Oppenheimer held views unpopular with the Air Force and certain AEC officials, and because he also wielded great influence politically and publicly, he posed a significant threat to his opposition's policies and programs. Their interests required Oppenheimer's removal from government service. Although the evidence for such an argument appears overwhelming, no interpretation is absolute. Certainly, a complex of forces led to Oppenheimer's 1954 security hearing.

THE CRISIS YEARS: OPPENHEIMER FALTERS AGAINST THE "BLANK WALL"

Neither Oppenheimer nor later political analysts were surprised that Oppenheimer was not reappointed to the AEC general advisory committee when his term expired in 1952. He and two other scientists, who also were deposed, had expressed views inconsistent with those of both the Truman and the Eisenhower administrations. While Oppenheimer continued as director of Princeton's Institute for Advanced Study, only a two-year consulting contract linked him with the government. In November 1952, the first hydrogen bomb was exploded, a clear indication that views similar to Oppenheimer's no longer led science or government. In December 1952, the AEC chairman, Gordon Dean, and commissioner, Lewis Strauss (one of Oppenheimer's long-time adversaries), confiscated Oppenheimer's classified files, all thirty-two feet of them. At this time, Oppenheimer, though obviously waning in influence, still maintained his security clearance.

While the confiscation of Oppenheimer's files remained relatively quiet, in May 1953, the rumblings against Oppenheimer began to surface publicly. An anonymous *Fortune* magazine article accused Oppenheimer, along with three other scientists, of a conspiracy to thwart U.S. security. The author suggested that "a life-and-death struggle over national military policy has developed between a highly influential group of American scientists and the military. . . . The prime mover among the scientists is . . . Dr. J. Robert Oppenheimer."[22] The article listed several of Oppenheimer's advisory recommendations as evidence of his conspiratorial motives: the hydrogen bomb decision; a recommendation to divert nuclear resources from strategic to tactical weapons; and his support of development of continental air defenses, among others. The author even named the conspiracy ZORC, for its supposed members—Jerrold Zacharias, Oppenheimer, Rabi, and Charles Lauritsen. Once again, timing complicated Oppenheimer's situation. The *Fortune* article appeared only days before *Foreign Affairs* magazine carried one of Oppenheimer's speeches, and his words fueled his opposition's arsenal. He had said, "The very least we can conclude is that our twenty-thousandth bomb . . . will not in any deep strategic sense offset their two-thousandth."[23] In the meantime, the Soviets detonated a thermonuclear device, years ahead of the estimate by the AEC general advisory committee; ironically, Oppenheimer had been the committee chairman when the faulty forecast was made. The sentiment that surrounded Oppenheimer within government circles in the early 1950s was far from favorable, and was deteriorating.

The general political climate in 1954 threatened Oppenheimer as well. By that date, both the United States and the Soviet Union had demonstrated atomic and thermonuclear power. Although the Soviet Union's ability to make a usable weapon was still questionable, the threat was real. The Cold War ideology quickly followed. The East-West standoff clearly showed that Oppenheimer's calls for international control and shared scientific knowledge, made a decade earlier, were faded ideals. Additionally, McCarthyism increased Oppenheimer's vulnerability. Only intercession by the then vice president, Richard Nixon, saved Oppenheimer from investigation by the House Un-American Activities Committee.[24]

The country's "communist paranoia" prompted President Eisenhower to enact Executive Order 10450 in April 1953. This order required a thorough investigation of all individuals seeking federal employment and included everyone already employed. By this order, reopening Oppenheimer's FBI dossier could be considered merely procedural. Unfortunately for Oppenheimer, his two previous security clearances did not override the process, and his file fell into unfriendly hands.

The 7 November 1953 Borden letter to J. Edgar Hoover contained this summary:

1. Between 1939 and 1942, more probably than not, J. Robert Oppernheimer was a sufficiently hardened Communist that he either volunteered espionage information to the Soviets, or complied with a request for such information.

2. More probably than not, he has since been functioning as an espionage agent; and

3. More probably than not, he has since acted under Soviet directive in influencing United States military, atomic energy, intelligence, and diplomatic policy.[25]

In response to Borden's charges, the FBI sent a report to the White House; to the AEC chairman, Strauss; and to the secretary of defense, Charles Wilson. On 4 December 1953, President Eisenhower ordered a "blank wall" placed between Oppenheimer and all classified information. The president also directed the U.S. attorney general to recommend appropriate action after thorough investigation. The AEC decided the next week to "institute regular procedures" to determine the veracity of Borden's charges.

The first step was the presentation of charges to Oppenheimer, accomplished in the letter from Nichols, which Nichols and Commissioner Strauss presented to Oppenheimer on 21 December 1953. On 4 March 1953, Oppenheimer replied with a letter that answered Nichols's charges and requested a hearing before the Personnel Security Board.

As Oppenheimer prepared his defense, public events worked against him. On 17 March 1954, only two weeks after Oppenheimer requested a hearing, the success of Operation Castle was announced. The United States had tested a usable hydrogen bomb. The superbomb was news.[26]

The Castle series produced unprecedented results. Not only was a practical weapon tested, but that weapon's explosive potential was shown to be incredible. Headlines on March 18 declared, "2nd Hydrogen Blast Proves Mightier Than Any Forecast."[27] After days of official silence, President Eisenhower confirmed that the hydrogen blast had been much bigger than anticipated. Even the scientists were surprised by its magnitude.

Eisenhower and Commissioner Strauss attempted to reassure the American people that nuclear power was not "out of control." In an address to the nation, Eisenhower said that the only threat to the nation was "the great threat imposed upon us by aggressive communism."[28]

While the president tried to calm the public, Senator McCarthy fueled their fears. In a speech designed primarily to attack a journalist, Edward R. Murrow, McCarthy suggested that subversion within government had delayed the hydrogen bomb project by eighteen months. When asked about McCarthy's charge the next day, President Eisenhower denied any knowledge of such activity.

Whether Eisenhower knew fully the charges brought against Oppenheimer is unclear. And although Eisenhower denied any knowledge of the situation, a seed of suspicion was planted publicly by the press. The public might suspect scientists of wrongdoing. It was only a matter of time until the public was told that Oppenheimer was the potential "scientist villain."

In order to preempt further attacks by McCarthy, Oppenheimer released to the *New York Times* Nichols's letter of accusation and his own formal response. The investigation into Oppenheimer's life rocketed into the public agenda. Only five days later, Oppenheimer faced the Personnel Security Board for the first time. In the month between his reply to the derogatory information and the hearing's start, both communism and the hydrogen bomb had dominated the news. Oppenheimer's life was inextricably tied to both issues.

It is impossible to say what caused Oppenheimer's loss of security clearance, but the general situation that contributed to Oppenheimer's fall is known. It is appropriate, then, to look more deeply into the case itself—at the rhetoric that condensed the ideas presented by both sides, and at the choices of human action embedded within those words.

NOTES

1. Philip M. Stern, *The Oppenheimer Case: Security on Trial* (New York: Harper and Row, 1969), 8. Most historical information can be found in several sources. The notation in this chapter is used only to reflect unique information or interpretations of events.

2. "The Oppenheimer Hearings," *Bulletin of Atomic Scientists* 10 (1954): 234.

3. Nuel Pharr Davis, *Lawrence and Oppenheimer*, reprint of 1968 edition (New York: Da Capo, 1986), 23.

4. Ibid., 24.

5. Robert Jungk, *Brighter than a Thousand Suns: A Personal History of the Atomic Scientists* (New York: Harcourt, Brace, 1958), 178-80; and Ralph E. Lapp, *The New Priesthood: The Scientific Elite and the Uses of Power* (New York: Harper and Row, 1965), 48-49.

6. Joseph Haberer, *Politics and the Community of Science* (New York: Van Nostrand Reinhold, 1969), 221.

7. Hans Bethe, "Fermi Prize: J. Robert Oppenheimer Named to Receive Annual AEC Award," *Science*, 12 April 1963, 161.

8. Denise Royal, *The Story of J. Robert Oppenheimer* (New York: St. Martin's, 1969), 101-4.

9. Jungk, *Brighter than a Thousand Suns*, 181.

10. Ibid., 181-82.

11. Ibid., 127-28.

12. Ibid., 186.

13. Ibid., 203.

14. Thomas W. Wilson, Jr., *The Great Weapons Heresy* (Boston: Houghton Mifflin, 1970), 30.

15. Ibid., 47.

16. Robert Gilpin, *American Scientists and Nuclear Weapons Policy* (Princeton: Princeton University Press, 1962), 98.

17. Ibid., 99.

18. Ibid., 102-7.

19. Richard T. Sylves, *The Nuclear Oracles: A Political History of the General Advisory Committee of the Atomic Energy Commission, 1947-1977* (Ames: Iowa State University Press, 1987), 169.

20. Ibid., 170.

21. Herbert York, *The Advisors: Oppenheimer, Teller, and the Superbomb* (San Francisco: W. H. Freeman, 1976), 137-43; Sylves, *Nuclear Oracles*, 160-64.

22. "The Hidden Struggle for the H-Bomb: The Story of Dr. Oppenheimer's Persistent Campaign to Reverse the U.S. Military Strategy," *Fortune*, May 1953, 109.

23. J. Robert Oppenheimer, "Atomic Weapons and American Policy," *Foreign Affairs* 31 (1953): 525-35.

24. Stern, *Oppenheimer Case*, 204.

25. Quoted in Peter Goodchild, *J. Robert Oppenheimer: Shatterer of Worlds* (Boston: Houghton Mifflin, 1981), 223.

26. See Hanson W. Baldwin, "Atom Tests Emphasize Stepped-up Arms Race: New Series in Pacific Will Include First Operating Model of H-Bomb," *New York Times*, 7 March 1954, D5; and "Hydrogen Bomb Confirmed," *New York Times*, 17 March 1954, A9.

27. "2nd Hydrogen Blast Proves Mightier Than Any Forecast," *New York Times*, 18 March 1954: A1.

28. William L. Laurence, "Vast Power Bared: March 1 Explosion Was Equivalent to Millions of Tons of TNT," *New York Times*, 1 April 1954, A1.

Chapter 3

A Linguistic Calculus: Terminological Algebra

Oppenheimer's historical and political environment points to the factors that led to his 1954 security hearing: his communist associations, his early political naïveté, his later unpopular policy recommendations, and the international tension of the early 1950s. Historical and political explanations alone, however, fail to show why the accusations against Oppenheimer triumphed over his defense. Clearly, Oppenheimer was vulnerable, but at the same time, the Los Alamos mystique, his service record, and political precedent supported his position. A large group of prominent scientists, military officers, and politicians supported Oppenheimer as well. One purpose of this book is to explain why Oppenheimer's defense failed; in other words, the book explores the question of why one naming of Oppenheimer's acts was more acceptable to his judges than the other.

That critical goal raises several subordinate considerations. First, the Oppenheimer case documents "rewrote" Oppenheimer's life. As with any historical record, Nichols, Oppenheimer, and the judges chose particular and strategic terms to describe Oppenheimer's past. They used their terminologies to label Oppenheimer's acts. Once acts are labeled, the descriptive implications of the labels take on great importance. Burke notes that "much that we take as observations about 'reality' may be but the spinning out of the possibilities implicit in the particular choice of terms."[1] The terms chosen by Oppenheimer, Nichols, and the AEC judges, then, reflect their diverse and divergent perceptions about Oppenheimer's situation. A given terminology may reflect "reality" as the advocate sees it, but as Burke cautions, "by its very nature as a terminology it must be a selection of reality; and to that extent it must function also as a deflection of reality.''[2] Each Oppenheimer case document reflected, selected, and deflected reality. Some selections favored Oppenheimer; others did not. At conflict were two plausible realities, one for and one against Oppenheimer; in the judges' eyes, one of these would emerge as the most rhetorically probable. To understand how the parties in the Oppenheimer case made their "selections" and how these choices had implications for the outcome requires an exploration of each rhetoric's terminology and of the language motives revealed in these strategic language choices. Analysis of the case's rhetorical characteristics, then, requires a theoretical stand and an analytical method that focus on strategic language choice and terminological implications.

Second, the case calls for some means by which to explain the varying degrees of opposition revealed in language choice. Although each rhetor involved in the Oppenheimer case made judgments based on a single and shared pool of documented evidence, the three decisions evince very diverse explanations for Oppenheimer's dismissal. At points, the judges' estimations of the "facts" are diametrically opposed. At other points, Oppenheimer and his judges agree. On some issues, the judges disagree among themselves. Therefore, the method chosen to analyze the case not only must treat opposed descriptions of situations like those indicated above, but also must address the especially complex oppositional situations that exist among the multiple rhetors.

Third, the theory and method brought to this case also must explore key points of ambiguity, where meanings may be shared and condensed or diverse and diverging. For example, in the Oppenheimer case, words such as loyalty, security, and veracity were used both to support and to degrade Oppenheimer's actions. Burke notes that terms often condense experience. He submits that

any overall term for motivation, such as honor, loyalty, liberty, equality, fraternity, is a *summing up* of many motivational strands. And though on its face it reduces a whole complexity of terms to one apparently simple term, the people who used it may have been quite aware of many other meanings subsumed in it, but not explicitly proclaimed.[3]

Because all the Oppenheimer case rhetors used such overall terms, the method employed here must explore motivational strands implicit in the invocation of particular terms and in the explanations for action thereby implied.

Finally, the theory and method used here must consider the historical and political environment crucial to the case. The environment helps to establish the motivational strands implicit in terms, and thereby is necessary to the analysis as a whole. The case discourse, obviously, must be considered in context.

The public documents of the Oppenheimer case provide the evidence necessary to explore Oppenheimer's rhetorical failure, while Burke provides the theoretical orientation and the method required. Terminological algebra, a Burkean method developed and extended here, provides the lens through which a critic can examine the complexities of discursive evidence.

A THEORETICAL PRELUDE: LANGUAGE AS SYMBOLIC ACTION

Burke notes that a rhetorical critic's concern is "primarily with the analysis of language rather than with the analysis of 'reality.' Language being essentially human, we should view human relations in terms of the linguistic instrument."[4] Any verbal expression reflects, selects, and deflects reality. Each individual attends to certain events and overlooks others, sometimes consciously, sometimes unconsciously. The verbal expressions of these reflections, selections, and deflections is itself a form of action and is the basis for human "reality." Language is active because it involves and reflects human choice making and judgment. Individuals select and attend to certain stimuli and then choose the terms that encapsulate their observations. The terminology employed establishes some events as meaningful and others as insignificant. Language is symbolic action, not only because words are symbols, but also because language is representative in a larger sense. The words people choose to express their perceptions betray and display their particular world views. They state what for them is reality and act on the basis of that reality. William H. Rueckert, building on Burke's thought, suggest that rhetors create a "symbolic autobiography" in their verbalizations.[5] That autobiography is a socialized product, and language choices are sociological statements.

To understand and participate in their world, people invoke shared terms used to describe situations or patterns of experience. As interaction spreads throughout a group, terms begin to represent certain common events, experiences, and judgments. Each person builds what Burke calls an "orientation" or "a bundle of judgments as to how things were, how things are, and how they may be."[6] In turn, the terminologies that express orientations guide people in evaluation and explanation. Terminologies carry the "thou shalts" and "thou shalt nots" of society. Burke suggests that when individuals are asked to explain their actions, their immediate source is society's terminology. That terminology and its constitutive terms direct the interpretation and evaluation of acts.

In the society in which he was raised, there were prescribed and proscribed rules of conduct, and a terminology of motives to go with them. He was conditioned not only as regards what he should do and should not do, but also as regards the reasons for his acts. When introspecting to find the explanation for his attitudes he would naturally employ the verbalizations of his group—for what are his language and thought if not a socialized product? . . . One is simply interpreting with the only vocabulary he knows. One is stating his orientation, which involves a vocabulary of ought and ought not, with attendant vocabulary of praiseworthy and blameworthy.[7]

Because terminologies are linked to human choice making and the explanation of human action, terminologies inherently involve motive attribution. A motive is an explanation of human action. Motives are attributed, Burke believes, whenever anyone says what people are doing and why they are doing it. When someone provides an explanation for an action, those who hear the explanation "critically" assess or speculate about the motives of the speaker. This is accomplished when the terms invoked are treated as "shorthand" for the situation described. Motive attribution, therefore, is an interpretive act explicitly tied to a rhetor's terms and terminologies.

Therefore, from the critic's perspective, a rhetor's choice of terms implies accountability. Because symbolic actions involve choice from a range of alternative actions, the actors are always accountable for their choices. In some cases they may be called to account for the choices made. The labels attached to acts and the motives that the terms imply advise the available interpretations of the act. Terms implicate a rhetor's evaluations of a situation. So when Oppenheimer or his accusers spoke, the equivalent verbal motive attribution occurred; these "realities" were interpreted by the judges, and the terms invoked came to "stand for" the actions of each side.

Interpretation of reality and attribution of motives is possible because language choice situates action. For instance, if a soldier is observed running from the battle lines, several descriptive terms can be invoked: "desertion," "retreat," or "intelligent survivalist response." Each descriptor implies different motives, because interpretations of the soldier's actions are situated differently. Each term embodies a different meaningful relationship between the act (the run from battle) and a context. Desertion means that the soldier is running away in violation of military orders. The soldier is breaking regulations and may be called to account for the choice. The act, in a military terminology, is wrong and deserves punishment. Retreat, on the other hand, is acceptable and may be strategic. The running-away act, in this "survivalist" terminology, was part of a military plan. The soldier followed orders. Indeed, to defy an order to retreat usually warrants some accounting for the act. Should it become important to name the soldier's act, as in a citation ceremony or a court martial proceeding, the choice of "retreat" or "desertion" would be critical to the outcome, because terms not only advise evaluations, but inform the response to the act.

Although terminologies guide decision and action, they are not static. Social interaction constantly transforms the advice carried in terms and terminologies. The label "intelligent survivalist response" demonstrates the changeability of orientations and their terminologies. To Americans, naming the soldier's act an "intelligent survivalist response" would tend to defy the socially created terminology that surrounds military service. If enough people adopt the term, however, its appropriateness as a descriptor increases. If "intelligent survivalist response" should reach dominance as the descriptor of soldiers-running-from-battle events, the term would create a new context for the act; it would advise different, and perhaps less negative, responses to the act. Insofar as it is accepted by a group, the entitling term guides future evaluations and actions. The shift of meaning is possible because terminologies are as alive as the agents who create and employ them. They change and decay, sometimes at the urging of people with something at stake in the particular resolution of the situation.

Humans are social and so are their terms. Motive terms are sociological, because like their creators, they involve shared action and shared accounts for actions. Terms sometimes change as they are linked up with other terms and form clusters. Term A may mean one thing when clustered with terms B, C, and D and something quite different when in company with terms E, F, and G. The term "law and order" provides an example of changed meaning through clustering. Generally, law and order might mean the proper functioning of the judicial system, which includes police protection for citizens. More specific circumstances modify the term's context and consequently may produce a slightly different meaning. For example, for many Southerners during the 1960s, law and order meant keeping blacks in their places, with illegal force, if necessary. In the 1970s, frightened city dwellers used the term to justify vigilantism. And in the 1990s, the term "law and order" often is described as a code word for sanctioned discriminatory police practices. Law and order represents different motives in each case. Terms represent a person's or group's particular position on an issue.

Burke suggests that terms are of two types: "terms that put things together and terms that take things apart. Otherwise put, A can feel himself identified with B, or he can think of himself as dissociated from B."[8] Terms allow both composition and division of experiences. "All terminologies," in Burke's conception, "must implicitly or explicity embody choices between the principle of continuity and the principle of discontinuity."[9] Burke further explains a terminology's capacity to order experiences in this way: "One acts; in the course of acting one organizes the opposition to one's act (or in the course of asserting, one causes a multitude of counter-assertions to come running from all directions like outlaws in the antique woods converging upon the place where a horn sounded)."[10] Terms align the sides in a conflict, those for and those against. If accepted, discourse creates a particular view of reality, of right and wrong; this rhetoric indicates the "good guys" and "bad guys" and helps to achieve identification with one group or the other.

Burke's treatment of terms as action encompasses notions of opposition, ambiguity, motive, and accountability. The treatment situates language within a negotiable social context. In sum, language choice is identified as the avenue by which observers understand why people do things and why things turn out as they do. Since such is, in a general sense, the purpose of this book, Burke's linguistically based rhetorical theory allows fruitful examination of the Oppenheimer case.

Using the treatment of language as symbolic action as a theoretical basis for the approach to the Oppenheimer case, a method based in Burke's cluster-agon approach can now be identified.

Cluster-agon method requires a rigorous analysis of language choice. Burke actually terms this approach "statistical indexing." A linguistic analysis is statistical in that it is an analysis of a population's characteristics (the rhetor's thought and motive) by inference from a sample (the rhetor's language choices). It is an index because the inferred characteristics "serve to guide, point out, or otherwise facilitate reference" to the rhetor's thought/motives.[11] To form the index, Burke recommends that a rhetorical critic perform a microscopic analysis of a rhetor's language. Language choice should be observed carefully to discern the representative, characteristic equations embedded in the text. These discovered equations form a motivational index for the particular rhetor.

The work of every writer contains a set of implicit equations. He uses "associational clusters." And you may, by examining his work, find "what goes with what" in these clusters—what kinds of acts and images and personalities and situations go with his notions of heroism, villainy, consolation, despair, etc. . . . Afterwards, by inspecting his work "statistically," we or he may disclose by objective citation the structure of motivation operating here.[12]

Burke directs the critic to look for more than "what goes with what." He also points to two structural equations: (1) progression, or "from what through what to what," noted as

$$\underline{\quad} \rightarrow \underline{\quad} \rightarrow \underline{\quad}$$

and (2) equality, instances when terms are mutually reinforcing, presented as

$$\underline{\quad} = \underline{\quad}$$

Opposition, or the agon, "what is vs. what," is noted with a slanted line between terms, thus:

$$\underline{\quad} / \underline{\quad}^{13}$$

Burke reinforces his statistical method with this caution: "We should watch for 'critical points' within the work, as well as at beginnings and endings. There are often 'watershed moments,' changes of slope, where some new quality enters.''[14] Above all, a critic must let the discourse unveil equations. Equations are not created; they are discovered. The statistical method requires "objective citation" to support the critic's proposed equations.[15]

A statistical perspective and objective citation do not mean that the method itself is empirically objective. Cluster-agon analysis is subjective; the equations are interpretations. Burke's symbolic index is not meant to be used like a dictionary of language-choice implications; on the contrary, the index is intended to apply only to a particular rhetor and usually to a particular work. Equations, Burke cautions, always must be related to context. They are not immutable structures, alike in all discourse. Each equational interpretation is specific to the analyzed discourses. While similar equations may exist in many diverse works, the similarity should not be imposed. Each discourse must be analyzed to make a valid generalization.

Armin Paul Frank assimilates Burke's ideas, cautioning the reader to watch for these occurrences:

(1) Conflict or opposition: what is the dramatic alignment? (2) Repetition: what, if any, are the equations? (3) Accumulation, or apposition: in what way do associational clusters agglutinate? Watch for dissimilarities as well as for similarities! (4) Progression: what are the transformations? (5) Implied in this question is what, if anything, is left behind?—an attenuated way of looking for what, in extreme forms, is the sacrifice and the kill.[16]

Beyond his somewhat dispersed presentation of the cluster-agon method's possibilities, Burke never clearly outlines a statistical indexing procedure. And criticism that uses the cluster-agon method adds only minimal guidance.

Cluster-agon requires painstaking analysis and relies heavily on the critic's ability to draw insight from the analysis. The method structures a critic's description of what is happening within discourse and hopefully points toward meaningful interpretations and evaluations. Unfortunately, while Rueckert, Carol A. Berthold, and others have systematized the cluster-agon method, they often fail to go beyond mere description.[17] Perhaps more problematic is the method's exposition. Berthold attempts to use graphics to demonstrate the relationships among terms, yet fails to indicate the terms' relative weights or the method's complexity beyond a single level. Similarly, Elizabeth Walker Mechling and Jay Mechling, in their article about anti-sugar rhetoric, identify equations but present no clear equational structures, either in prose or in graphics, to support their conclusions.[18] Burke's suggested equational forms are abandoned by these cluster-agon critics. Although a method should not overpower the discourse or the criticism presented, clear presentation of equations supports the critic's task and the reader's understanding.

As it has been used, not only does the cluster-agon method lack presentational flexibility beyond a single level, but the resultant analysis is also limited in scope. Berthold suggests that cluster-agon method could be used to compare the rhetoric of multiple, and even opposed, rhetors. Cluster-agon should reveal key issues or a conflict of "what is at issue" in most situations. Such studies, however, demand greater explanative complexity than present cluster-agon analysis has demonstrated. Language choices often involve layers of meaning, which must be exposed in order to reveal a rhetor's meaning fully. Once identified, the "layers" are difficult to present. If cluster-agon analysis and exposition is problematic with one speaker's discourse, its usefulness for multiple speakers is doubtful. The method, therefore, needs greater flexibility and sophistication that is equal to the task of presenting not only the complex language choices of a single rhetor, but those of multiple, opposed rhetors. Cluster-agon's problems of rigor, presentation, flexibility, and complexity can be solved by an extension and refinement I call "terminological algebra."

TERMINOLOGICAL ALGEBRA INTRODUCED

A solution to cluster-agon's inadequacies may rest, appropriately enough, in Burke's language choices. Recall that his method is called "statistical indexing," which can be defined loosely as a close examination of a rhetor's thought and motives by inference from a representative sample of the rhetor's language choices. Discourse serves as a data base from which the rhetorical statistician extrapolates explanations of human action. Moreover, Burke suggests that the extrapolations should be equations.

Equations, in an abstract sense, are symbolic statements about terminological relationships. Terminological algebra, the refinement and extensions of the cluster-agon method proposed here, returns to Burke's original suggestions for guidance. It outlines a terminological equation-building system, and it concentrates on careful analysis of terms in contexts and the relationships between the contextualized terms. The proposed terminological algebra might be understood best through its counterpart in the field of mathematics, numerical algebra.

Exposition of terminological algebra, as with its numerical equivalent, must begin with the units to be analyzed, in this case with terms. A "term" is more than "any word or group of words expressing a notion or denoting an object." It has been defined variously as "the condition or stipulation that defines the nature and limits of an agreement"; "the relation between two persons or groups; footing"; and "each of two concepts being compared or related in a proposition; specifically, each of the words or phrases constituting the subject and the predicate."[19] One might have "peace terms," be on "speaking terms," state a "major term" in a syllogism, or "come to terms" with someone else. In each case, terms involve some relationship of either persons to situations, persons to other persons, or ideas to ideas. In yet another sense, terms are "each of (two or more) quantities connected by the signs of addition or subtraction in an algebraic expression or equation."[20] Terms can be either words or numbers connected in relationships.

Within equations, both words and numbers function symbolically; they represent things and ideas. Perhaps Burke suggested "term equations" because terms, in the verbal sense, describe humans acting in situations, and equations, in any sense, are designed to collapse complex symbolic relationships into manageable and enlightening forms. Remember also that Burke believes that terms cluster; they promote composition of and division of experience. Burke, a master of puns, tempts a rhetorical scholar to rephrase his ideas so that terms are added together, rather than clustered. Clusters also might be broken down and parts subtracted from the cluster to transform it. Perhaps it is far from coincidental that the Latin root of the term "algebra" means "the science of reuniting."[21] In mathematics and also in the terminological perspective proposed here, the clear presentation of complex relationships is central. Both algebras are "a calculus of symbols combining according to certain defined laws."[22] The terminological laws, which will be outlined in this section, make possible the greater rigor required of this extension of cluster-agon method.

The symbolic parallel between linguistic terms and numerical terms also enables terminological algebra to uncover the values embedded in terms. A value may be broadly considered the worth of something. Value may also be defined as "the precise meaning or import, as of a carefully considered word" or as "the precise number or amount represented by a figure."[23] Both numbers and words are symbols that represent the quality of some quantity. Numbers stand for numerical values. Language expresses "human values," those "ideas or relationships which people accord worth, usefulness, or importance."[24] In mathematical equations, the terms' values may be added or subtracted in order to find the value of an unknown. A similar process may be observed in language. Just as 3 is greater than 2, a person's human values carry varying weights. The words that express those values can either outweigh or be outweighed by other terms. A person's love of country (value of patriotism) might outweigh the same person's belief that to kill is unforgivable (value of human life). Since terms carry values in relation to evaluation and judgment, their comparison in equations should highlight their relative weights, just as numerical equations highlight the value relationships between numbers.

Like numerical algebra, the addition and subtraction of terminological values, then, may be used to determine the values of critical unknowns. The goal of numerical algebra is to approximate the value of an x, an unknown. Terminological algebra follows a similar goal—to establish the unknown meanings and values held by particular terms in a rhetor's terminology.

Terminological algebra considers unknown terminological values in an attempt to preserve the cluster-agon method's ability to analyze ambiguous and complicated language choices. This book focuses on the unknowns that the Personnel Security Board was convened to identify: What was a security risk, and did Oppenheimer fall within that definition? Because of its emphasis on terminological values, terminological algebra should unravel the ambiguities of the Oppenheimer case.

Terminological algebra provides a means to uncover human values hidden in ambiguity because it translates numerical algebra's simple, yet sophisticated, symbol system into the verbal realm. Terminological algebra treats words or phrases as terms in situation-defining and situation-clarifying equations. As in numerical algebra, the principle of substitution allows presentation of term clusters in either "lowest terms" or at their most complicated level. Burke notes that the cluster-agon method (and therefore terminological algebra, as its extension) relies on the principle of synecdoche.

We consider synecdoche to be the basic process of representation, as approached from the standpoint of "equations" or "what goes with what." To say that one can substitute the part for whole, whole for part, container for the thing contained, thing contained for the container, cause for effect, or effect for cause, is simply to say that both members of these pairs belong in the same associational cluster.[25]

In numerical algebra, the simple equation

$$2 + 2 = 4$$

could be transformed through substitution to

$$(-21 + 23) + (12 - 10) = 1 + 3$$

The equation's total meaning has not changed. However, to break down the terms is to find out how 4 was attained from the infinite possibilities available. That also is the task of rhetorical analysis—to find the explanations of particular terms, to find out how a rhetor arrives at a particular "naming" from the many terminological possibilities available. Thus, terminological algebra adopts numerical algebra's principles of composition, division, and substitution of terms. In doing so, the critic may be better equipped to delve into hidden meanings without distorting the equation's original, seemingly simple, meaning. A critic may examine clusters within clusters within clusters. And, as with numerical algebra, terminological algebra suggests a way to present the discovered equations in all their complexity or simplicity.

Once a critic learns terminological algebra's symbol system, almost any terminological relationship can be charted clearly. Diagrams like those used by Berthold and Laura Crowell failed to show the relationships between terms and the terms' weights. Terminological algebra incorporates both of these key cluster factors into the symbol system itself. The charting of equations suggested in terminological algebra may be as helpful to the reader as to the critic.

Terminological algebra is an attempt to systematize cluster-agon method more thoroughly and to overcome the method's problems of rigor, flexibility and complexity, and presentation. Its analogous relationship with numerical algebra bodes well. The following are the central tenets of the methodological extension.

Axiom 1: Terms that are used interchangeably or as synonyms are treated as equivalent terms.

Burke notes that "if a term notably appears and reappears in connection with some other term, we can begin to build up equations whereby the terms are treated as overlapping in their jurisdiction, and maybe even sometimes identical."[26] The critic should consider synonyms and interchangeable terms equivalent, and should note that relationship with an equals sign between the terms, as Burke suggests.

Terms may be equivalent both literally and figuratively. For example, the terms "teacher," "educator," and "tutor" may be used interchangeably in most situations. Their resultant equivalency will be represented as:

$$\text{teacher} = \text{educator} = \text{tutor}$$

The Declaration of Independence also provides an example of equivalent terms. In three separate instances, the authors refer to England's treatment of the Colonies as "abuses and usurpations," "injuries and usurpations," and "oppressions."[27] From these references, a critic might note several equivalencies. First, because of their interchangeable position in regard to "usurpations," "abuses" and "injuries" appear equivalent. The longer terms "abuses and usurpations," "injuries and usurpations," and "oppressions" also are equivalent, since all three terms refer to the same list of grievances. Written algebraically, the equivalencies are:

$$\text{abuses} = \text{injuries}$$

and

$$(\text{abuses and usurpations}) = (\text{injuries and usurpations}) = \text{oppressions}$$

Note that two or more words may comprise a single term. For clarity, such instances will be set apart with parentheses. If further separation or grouping of terms is required, brackets also will be used.

Figurative terms also indicate equivalencies. If a rhetor consistently identifies an idea or object through metaphor or analogy, the analogous terms should be considered equivalent. For instance, the former Soviet Union often was pictured or referred to through a bear's image. Such terms, then, present a figurative equivalency and will be represented as:

Bear = Soviet Union

Lincoln's "A House Divided" speech betrays a figurative equivalency in its title. Early in the speech, Lincoln said: "A house divided against itself cannot stand. I believe this government cannot endure permanently half slave and half free." Later in the speech, he spins out the metaphor:

when we see a lot of framed timbers, different portions of which we know have been gotten out at different times and places and by different workmen . . . and when we see these timbers joined together, and see they exactly make the frame of a house or a mill, all the tenons and mortises exactly fitting, and all the lengths and proportions of the different pieces exactly adapted to their respective places.[28]

The most obvious equivalency in this example is the metaphor between the house and the government, thus:

divided house = troubled U.S. government

Within this broad metaphorical equivalency, each part of the house and each of its architects might be equated with an actual government agency and government official. The equivalencies may be as elaborate as the rhetor's language choice demands.

Axiom 2: A concept consistently considered as two or more definitive terms comprises a compository cluster.

In concert with Burke's emphasis on composition and clusters, terminological algebra uses addition to note "what goes with what." For example, suppose term A consistently is broken down into component terms (issues) B, C, and D. The relationship will be noted algebraically as:

$$A = B + C + D$$

The compository terms B, C, and D are both necessary and sufficient to the meaning of A. As in numerical algebra, the additive terms together form the total, A.

The concept "volume" might clarify the compository cluster. Volume requires consideration of each of three component terms: length, width, and height. If a dimension is missing, the volume cannot be determined. The conceptional relationship in terminological form is represented as:

$$\text{volume} = \text{length} + \text{width} + \text{height}$$

While the analogy between numerical algebra and terminological algebra is illustrated by this axiom, the analogy should not be overextended. Note that the numerical equation for volume uses multiplication:

$$\text{volume} = \text{length} \times \text{width} \times \text{height}$$

Numbers would be substituted for the words in order to solve the equation. When volume is considered terminologically, however, the relationship involves addition. This example demonstrates that, although terminological algebra is similar to numerical algebra, it is also an autonomous calculus. Its rules are separate and independent of all other similar symbolic systems.

The Declaration of Independence provides yet another, perhaps better known, terminological example. Probably every American grade school graduate knows the sentence, "We hold these Truths to be self-evident, that all Men are created equal, that they are endowed by their Creator with certain unalienable Rights, that among these are Life, Liberty, and the Pursuit of Happiness."[29] Among other things, this sentence presents a compository cluster. "Unalienable rights" is defined in terms of life, liberty, and the pursuit of happiness. The cluster is presented, then, as:

$$\text{some unalienable rights} = \text{life} + \text{liberty} + \text{pursuit of happiness}$$

Earlier, compository terms were defined as "necessary and sufficient." In the example given here, the words "among these" suggest that the compository terms are neither necessary nor sufficient. However, of all available alternatives, the document's authors chose these particular examples. Barring further discourse or an interview, they are the only compository terms given to the hearer or reader. Their necessity and sufficiency are qualified by the particular context in which they are used.

Axiom 3: Terms that present the negative of, or are in some way opposed to, other terms are considered oppositional terms.

Terms promote composition, but they create division as well. Every "thou shalt" implies the possibility of a "thou shalt not." Many clusters also imply an agon. As Burke suggests, a critic should watch for "what is vs. what," or dramatic alignment. One indication of opposition is negation; signs of "this, not that" may exist in both the sentence structure and the rhetor's general ideas. Incompatible ideas or terms, or in more extreme cases, mutually exclusive ideas or terms, promote opposition. Instances where one term negates or opposes another term will be noted here as oppositional terms. The opposition will be noted as $A \neq B$ (A does not equal B, or A is not B).

Once oppositional terms are identified, they may be rounded out with oppositional compository clusters. An oppositional compository cluster is different from a compository cluster only in that it defines an oppositional term. In fact, the difference between a compository cluster and an oppositional compository cluster is of little note once an entire equation is built. The following example may clarify this point.

The opening paragraphs of Richard A. Viguerie's *The New Right* provide terminological contrasts typical of opposition.

The left is old and tired. The New Right is young and vigorous. Most of the liberals' leaders of the past 30 years are gone. . . . Our leaders are mostly in their 30's and 40's. The liberals had a lot of victories over the last 50 years. But they've grown soft and sluggish. We're lean and hungry—to gain victories for conservatism and to renew America. . . . We conservatives have a vision about the future. . . . We look forward, not backward, to the realization of the American dream. . . . The liberals have not only lost confidence in themselves but in their ideas.[30]

These paragraphs set up an opposition between liberals and conservatives and define the overarching positions through associated terminological clusters. Algebraically, the terminological relationship may be represented as an opposition:

$$\text{liberals} \neq \text{conservatives}$$

The description of each group then provides a cluster that fills out the group title. In Viguerie's terminology, liberals are old and tired, soft and sluggish, and backward-looking. Conservatives are the opposite: young and vigorous, lean and hungry, forward-looking. The clusters could be represented algebraically in various configurations:

$$\text{liberals} = (\text{old \& tired}) + (\text{soft \& sluggish}) + (\text{backward-looking})$$

$$\text{conservatives} = (\text{young \& vigorous}) + (\text{lean \& hungry}) + (\text{forward-looking})$$

Through substitution, the compositional clusters could define the equation's oppositional relationships. To highlight or explore the implications of particular terminological elements, the critic might represent particular elements of opposition:

$$\text{liberals} \neq \text{conservatives}$$

$$(\text{old \& tired}) \neq (\text{young \& vigorous})$$

The critic manipulates the equations to emphasize elements for critical analysis and explanation.

Axiom 4: Terms that call for, point to, or indicate the presence of other terminological relationships but do not form either equivalencies, clusters, or oppositions are identified as progressive terms.

Burke notes instances where a term's presence foretells the coming of another term or idea. In terminological algebra, such terms are called "progressive terms." Progressive terms typically note cause-effect, effect-cause, or other temporal or logical relationships. "Pregnancy" and "birth" are progressive terms because pregnancy carries with it the expectation of birth. Likewise, many archetypal forms are progressive: birth-death-rebirth; winter-spring-summer-autumn; dark-light; war-peace. While these terms may entail progressions in and of themselves, the structure of the discourse may also indicate progressions. Transitional material often uses terms that lead to other terms. A progressive terminological relationship is noted with an arrow between the progressive terms; this is the equational form that Burke originally proposed.

Burke suggests that a narrative work, especially, might require a "sign of sequence" such that

$$\text{event A} \rightarrow \text{event B} \rightarrow \text{event C}^{31}$$

Such progressions are crucial to the dramatic principle of plot. From this equation, the reader infers that event A leads to event B leads to event C. For example, almost any journalistic account of an event would give a step-by-step developmental explanation. The sequence could be noted algebraically with terms (steps) connected by arrows. The organizing process undertaken by the journalist creates a particular perspective on the event. If the lines are drawn differently within the sequence, resulting judgments about causes, time, and results may also change. However, the progressions may be more subtle than a recounting of events. The famous "I Have a Dream" speech by Martin Luther King, Jr., creates a temporal sequence from "yesterday's injustice" to "today's faith" to "tomorrow's hope and freedom." After describing the injustices of America's past and his dream for all African-Americans, King points to the future:

With this faith we will be able to hew out of the mountain of despair a stone of hope. With this faith, we will be able to transform the jangling discords of our nation into a beautiful symphony of brotherhood. With this faith, we will be able to work together, to pray together, to struggle together, to go to jail together, to stand up for freedom together, knowing that we will be free one day.[32]

King's words do not suggest that "faith" is equal to "freedom" or that "freedom" is part of "faith." If either case were true, the relationship between the terms would be equivalent or compository, respectively. King's words do suggest that "faith" will lead to "freedom." The entire section, then, in algebraic symbolism, could be encapsulated by a single equation:

$$faith \rightarrow freedom$$

Similar progressions surround any forecast. An economic forecast, for example, relies on many indicators. The indicators do not make up the ultimate forecast; rather, they lead to it. If housing starts lead to a forecast for economic growth, the relationship might be noted as:

$$high\ housing\ starts \rightarrow economic\ growth$$

Progressions may note any temporal context that clarifies the meaning of language choices.

These four axioms comprise terminological algebra's proposed compositional and divisional rules. To this point, however, the terminological algebraic system has dealt only with "known" relationships between terms and not specifically with terminological "unknowns" or with terminological value. The following principles address terminological unknowns and value weights.

Principle 1: Terminologies inherently involve choice and accountability, and therefore may be called into account.

Terminologies, by their nature, choose some events as meaningful and pass off other events as insignificant. Since choice is necessarily involved in verbal expression, rhetors are accountable for their terminologies. While always accountable, rhetors are only sometimes called to account for their choice of terms.

Richard Nixon, for instance, used a particular term, "executive privilege," to explain his withholding of information from the Watergate prosecutors. His explanation might have been accepted; in this case, however, the rhetor was called to account for his terminological choice and his executive privilege was questioned. Any case in which a term is questioned will be noted in terminological algebra with a question mark. In Nixon's situation, the term "executive privilege" would be noted as "(?executive privilege)." After further explanation, the term might be assigned a positive or negative value. The assignment of value will be discussed under Principle 3.

A terminological relationship may also be questioned. For instance, if Viguerie's liberal/conservative dichotomy is questioned, his equations can be noted as:

liberal ? conservative

conservatives ? (young & vigorous) + (lean & hungry) + (forward-looking)

These questioned terms and terminological relationships generally promote further discourse. The generated discussion, then, supplants and clarifies that which was questioned. Because of ongoing terminological negotiation, question marks will appear in terminological analysis.

Within every equation, terms carry values that indicate their varied and
relative weights in a rhetor's terminology. Terms have two types of value.
One terminological value indicates a term's force relative to other terms.
The second type of terminological value, ethical value, defines a term as
good or bad, positive or negative, a "thou shalt" or a "thou shalt not" in
the rhetor's orientation. Two weighting schemes, therefore, are proposed,
to address both possible terminological values.

*Principle 2: Terminologies are structured hierarchically according to
significance.*

Rhetoric reveals a hierarchy of terminological significance. Words such
as "key," "crucial," and "most importantly" place some terms in more
significant or "weighty" positions than other terms. While the phrase
"not only . . . but also" indicates parallel terms, phrases such as "more
important than these" or "on the next level" denote a hierarchical terminological ordering. For example, the apostle Paul, in his first letter to the
Corinthians, places the terms "faith," "hope," and "love" and their term
clusters into a hierarchy.

All the special gifts and power from God will someday come to an end, but love goes
on forever. Someday prophecy, and speaking in unknown languages, and special
knowledge—these gifts will disappear. . . . There are three things that
remain—faith, hope, and love—and the greatest of these is love. . . . Let love be
your greatest aim; nevertheless, ask also for the special abilities of the Holy Spirit
and the gift of prophecy, being able to preach the messages of God.[33]

Paul indicates explicitly that "love" holds the dominant position over its
associated terms, "faith" and "hope." The phrase, "Let love be your
greatest aim" also gives "love" priority over the special abilities of the Holy
Spirit and the prophetic gifts in God's revealed terminology.

Just as the rhetor's explicit statements establish a terminological hierarchy of significance, context also may indicate significance. Recall that
Burke calls for careful analysis of "watershed moments." He emphasizes
the need for critical sensitivity. For example, Burke says that "if a man
talks dully of *glory*, but brilliantly employs the imagery of *desolation*, his
true subject is *desolation*."[34] To assign terminological weights requires that

attention be given to the particular term, to the other terms attached to it, and to its meaning in a larger context.

Significant weights, once identified, will be symbolized in two ways. A term that is given priority over other terms in its cluster might be said to be "greater than" its associated terms. Thus it may be shown as $A > B$. If A outweighs both B and C in a cluster, the inequality will be shown as $A > B + C$. A second representational method will capitalize significant terms. For instance,

$$Y = A + b + c$$

indicates that in the definitive cluster of a, b, and c, a holds the greatest significance in the meaning of Y. The choice between "greater than" or capitalization depends on the particular equation's complexity and on the critic's explanatory goal.

Returning to the Biblical "love" example, the relationships among faith, hope, and love could be represented as:

$$\text{remaining gifts} = \text{LOVE} + \text{faith} + \text{hope}$$

or

$$\text{love} > \text{faith}; \text{love} > \text{hope}$$

Again, the equational representation that best explains the terminology should be used.

Principle 3: Terms carry differing ethical values.

A rhetor's terms often carry strong negative or positive ethical implications. Berthold's use of god- and devil-terms suggests an ethical opposition between key terms but unfortunately circumvents an important part of cluster-agon analysis. Although oppositional or agon terms, what Berthold calls devil-terms, often carry negative implications, terms may be opposed without being ethically opposed. For example, the maxim, "You can't have your cake and eat it, too," presents an opposition. Having a cake and eating the same cake are mutually exclusive acts. The conditions cannot exist simultaneously. Nevertheless, both acts are positive; indeed, the phrase is used to highlight situations in which a person must make a choice between two positive, but mutually exclusive, conditions. The situation is a positive-positive opposition. Likewise, rhetors may describe situations that force a choice between "two evils." Phrases like "pay me now or pay me later" communicate a negative-negative opposition.

Terminological algebra attempts to allow the critic flexibility to analyze these multiple terminological situations. Quite simply, if a rhetor proposes or uses a term as "good" or "positive" or "desired," the critic indicates the evaluation with a plus sign (+love). Likewise, a negative evaluation is designated by a minus sign (−dishonesty). Once again, the critic must interpret value statements and contextual meaning in order to assign a term's ethical value.

The critic may use the two weighting schemes proposed here in conjunction. Consider the following hypothetical example and the various equational configurations that emerge from the terminologies of different rhetors' language choices. Suppose that three individuals are given the opportunity to win a large sum of money. The only condition imposed on the reward is that each person must lie in order to receive the cash. Several responses are possible. A person, for instance, might respond, "I'm really not in the habit of telling lies, but money is money. I'll lie." The person reveals that both honesty and wealth are valued positively, and that wealth outweighs honesty in this case. The stated terminological relationships could be represented like this:

+ honesty
+ wealth
+ wealth > + honesty

A second person, presented with the same opportunity, might enact slightly different terminological relationships. That person might say, "Although the offer is tempting—everybody could use more money—I cannot lie." This person also values both honesty and wealth, but reverses the first person's weighting for significance. In this scenario, honesty outweighs wealth. The equations therefore look like this:

+ honesty
+ wealth
+ honesty > + wealth

Finally, consider the individual who feels that money is an evil, corrupting force and also believes that a person should not lie. Given the same opportunity to win money, this person, like the second person, would refuse to lie but explain that choice with a different terminology. "Wealth" receives a negative value initially. The equations that represent this person's terminology differ from the previous configurations:

+ honesty
− wealth
+ honesty > − wealth

Note that in each instance one cannot assume that one term outweighs the other based on ethical value. An equational scale recognizes only significance as force or influence. The ethical value shows whether the identified forceful term is good or bad in the rhetor's expressed orientation. This is a point where terminological algebra and numerical algebra diverge. In numerical algebra, positive and negative values necessarily counterbalance. In terminological algebra, positive and negative values are "significant" only after the relationship between and among terms is defined in that particular terminology. Terminological algebra is primarily concerned with absolute value, or rhetorical force. The separation may seem artificial, because in many terminologies a term gains significance because it is good. But an equal force may just as easily be felt in the opposite direction. The dual weighting system proposed here does not assume a link between goodness and influence.

Terminological algebra provides the critic a means to address both the predictable and the unusual. Terminological algebra encourages the critic to identify points of ambiguity, and therefore potential transformation, in a rhetor's discourse. Through mapping of terminological equations, the critic may notice shifts in terminological alliances, weights, and evaluations. A shift of a key term from one cluster to another, an unusual union of previously opposed terms, or a division in once united clusters all may indicate significant shifts in human attributions of motives and the creation of new orientations to situations. Any and all of these moves are the creation, transformation, or dissolution of political reality. Terminological algebra allows the critic and others literally to see the rhetorical moves that constitute political change. The value of the method will be demonstrated in the analysis of the Oppenheimer case that begins in Chapter 4.

NOTES

1. Kenneth Burke, *Language as Symbolic Action: Essays on Life, Literature, and Method* (Berkeley: University of California Press, 1966), 46.

2. Ibid., 45.

3. Kenneth Burke, *A Rhetoric of Motives* (Berkeley: University of California Press, 1969), 110.

4. Kenneth Burke, *A Grammar of Motives*, reprint of 1945 edition (Berkeley: University of California Press, 1969), 317.

5. William H. Rueckert, *Kenneth Burke and the Drama of Human Relations*, 2d ed. (Berkeley: University of California Press, 1982), 59.

6. Kenneth Burke, *Permanence and Change: An Anatomy of Purpose*, 3rd ed. (Berkeley: University of California Press, 1984), 14.

7. Ibid., 20.

8. Burke, *Language as Symbolic Action*, 49.

9. Ibid., 50.

10. Ibid., 367.

11. *American Heritage Dictionary of the English Language*, s.v. "index."

12. Kenneth Burke, *The Philosophy of Literary Form,* 3d ed. (Berkeley: University of California Press, 1973), 69.

13. Ibid., 75-77.

14. Ibid., 78.

15. Ibid., 20-21.

16. Armin Paul Frank, *Kenneth Burke* (New York: Twayne, 1969), 118.

17. See Ruekert, *Kenneth Burke*, 83-111, 163-91; Carol A. Berthold, "Kenneth Burke's Cluster-Agon Method: Its Development and an Application," *Central States Speech Journal* 17 (1976): 302-9; Laura Crowell, "Three Sheers for Kenneth Burke," *Quarterly Journal of Speech* 63 (1977): 152-77; Candiss Baksa Vibbert, "The Supreme Court and Obscenity: The Judicial Opinion as Rhetorical Reconstitution," Ph.D. diss., University of Iowa, 1981. Vibbert's dissertation is the best example of the interpretations and critical insights that rigorous cluster-agon analysis may generate.

18. Elizabeth Walker Mechling and Jay Mechling, "Sweet Talk: The Moral Rhetoric against Sugar," *Central States Speech Journal* 34 (1983): 19-32.

19. *The Compact Version of the Oxford English Dictionary* (New York: Oxford University Press, 1971), 3264.

20. Ibid., 3265.

21. Ibid., 55.

22. Ibid. The first readily understandable text on algebra was written by a nineteenth-century Islamic mathematician, Khwarzimi. The title, roughly translated, means "the art of bringing together unknowns to match a known quantity." The word "algebra" can be traced to the Arabic *al-jabr*, which means "the binding together of disorganized parts." See Desmond Steward, *Early Islam* (New York: Time-Life, 1967), 123, 128.

23. *Oxford English Dictionary*, 3586.

24. Ibid.

25. Burke, *Philosophy of Literary Form*, 77-78.

26. Burke, *Language as Symbolic Action*, 369.

27. Declaration of Independence, July 4, 1776, in Donald E. Cooke, *Our Nation's Great Heritage: The Story of the Declaration of Independence and the Constitution* (Maplewood, NJ: Hummond, 1972), 29.

28. "Lincoln's House Divided Speech: Springfield, Illinois, June 17, 1858," in Commager, ed., *Documents of American History*, vol. 1, p. 345.

29. Cooke, 29.

30. Richard A. Viguerie, *The New Right: We're Ready to Lead* (Falls Church, Va.: Viguerie Company, 1980), 1-2.

31. Burke, *Philosophy of Literary Form*, 75.

32. Martin Luther King, Jr., "I Have A Dream," in Wil A. Linkugel, R. R. Allen, and Richard L. Johannesen, eds., *Contemporary American Speeches*, 4th edition (Dubuque, Iowa: Wadsworth, 1978), 365.

33. 1 Corinthians 13:8-13, *The Living Bible, Paraphrased* (Wheaton, Ill.: Tyndale, 1971), 925.

34. Kenneth Burke, *Attitudes toward History*, 3d ed. (Berkeley: University of California Press, 1984), 233.

Chapter 4

Oppenheimer's Public Life Revisited: Analysis of the Accusations and the Defense

On 23 December 1953, General Nichols delivered a letter to Oppenheimer. On the surface, the letter was to inform Oppenheimer that the AEC had suspended his security clearance, present the reasons for the suspension, and offer Oppenheimer the opportunity to challenge the AEC's decision through a personnel security hearing. At the strategic level, however, the letter was intended to lay the groundwork for what proved to be one of the most famous security hearings in the nation's history, and as such, it was a carefully crafted accusation that called Oppenheimer's professional career and his character into question.

Nichols accepted a significant rhetorical challenge when the AEC asked him to suspend Oppenheimer's security clearance. Oppenheimer was one of the best known and most admired scientists in the nation. No matter how the accusations were framed, the nation, and especially the scientific community, would be shocked. Oppenheimer's popularity alone made the case a potential political powder keg. A second concern would be the possible counteraccusations against the AEC, which Nichols would need to preempt. Oppenheimer's alliance with the "finite containment" nuclear weapons philosophy was well known, both within government and to the general public. Any attack on him could be interpreted as an attempt by "infinite containment" advocates to eliminate the vocal opposition. To identify someone as a "security risk" due to support of an unpopular policy was unjust at best, and could easily be labeled undemocratic. Nichols's accusations must focus clearly on Oppenheimer's personal character and trustworthiness, not on the quality of his advice. Given Oppenheimer's past, McCarthy's "red scare" offered both an opportunity and a threat to the AEC in this regard. The growing concern about Communists within the United States made Oppenheimer's record especially troublesome. At the same time, to investigate Oppenheimer in 1954, after two earlier clearances, might seem more opportunistic than legitimate. The AEC could be accused of using the smokescreen created by McCarthyism to hide political motives. Accordingly, Nichols's rhetorical challenge was substantial.

At a theoretical level, Nichols faced the same rhetorical challenges central to any other accusation against character. Anyone who attempts to ascertain what motivates another suffers from the inability to see directly into the other's heart and mind and therefore must seek other avenues into the person's character. Scholars traditionally have suggested two ways to make judgments about an individual's character: the ends that the person pursues, as indicated through that person's acts, and the value attached to social roles that the individual assumes.[1]

The first category places emphasis on an individual's acts and the purposes achieved through those acts. Burke suggests that the relationship between act and agent is central to attribution of motives.

The agent is an author of his acts, which are descended from him, being good progeny if he is wise, silly progeny if he is silly. And, conversely, his acts can make him or remake him in accordance with their nature. They would be his product and/or he would be theirs.[2]

Thus, good acts demonstrate good character and bad acts indicate bad character. Oppenheimer's personal and professional history could shed light on his character.

The "character equation" is further complicated when purpose is added to the motivational mix. Acts may be judged on face value, or they may be judged according to the purpose they achieve. Thus, what might be perceived as a bad act in and of itself (violence against another person, for instance) may be judged as good if the act serves a good purpose (to protect a helpless individual). The identified purpose may transform the act from one of violent aggression to one of courageous defense. Ends do justify means in some evaluations.

Not only may a determination of purpose transform acts, but scenic factors also may influence a determination of character. The social roles a person assumes, the scenes or contexts in which that person acts, may offer insight into intention, motivation, and character. Denise M. Bostdorff notes that "the notion of social roles corresponds, interestingly enough, with the concept of persona. Originally, the Latin term *persona* referred to the mask an actor wore on stage. Later the contemporary word "person" developed from the term. Thus, an audience may evaluate the character of a rhetor (person) through the value it attributes to the various masks or personae the rhetor publicly assumes."[3] Oppenheimer's performance in his roles of scholar, teacher, friend, husband, father, administrator, and advisor to government all might be used to reveal aspects of his character.

Yet Oppenheimer's acts, purposes, and social roles alone could not determine his status as a "security risk." These factors are meaningful only in relation to some standard of judgment. Richard E. Crable notes:

Given a world of ambiguity, the privilege of choice, and the burden of responsibility and guilt, humanity both basks and suffers in its freedom. At the same time that human beings are free to act, they are never certain that their acts are good, nor immune to the charge that their acts were wrong.[4]

Meaning and evaluation rest in the interpretation of acts in relation to society's standards of behavior.

Evaluation of human action is uncertain for several reasons. First, the standards through which humans judge each other shift according to the dreams, fears, beliefs, and values that guide the judges at any time. Judgment in times of scarcity may differ from evaluation during a more prosperous period. Laws, societal standards, and other ethical codes are as changeable as the people who create them.

Second, standards differ between and among judging groups. The ideologies that separate pro–gay rights and anti–gay rights groups result in extremely polarized evaluations of a single act. Conservatives and liberals differ dramatically in their thinking about the role of "family values" in political life. One group may perceive an individual as a moral leader, while a second group may consider the same person a corrupt opportunist. That person's acts and character need not change materially; the judges and their evaluative orientations are the changeable element.

Third, application of an evaluative standard to a particular act is not a scientific process but a rhetorical one, and varies according to the orientation and abilities of the judges. One jury may produce a verdict completely different from that rendered by a second, even though both groups make their decision based on the same laws and the same facts. Their judgment is an interpretation and evaluation.

Ethical determinations, as Crable explains, do not rest solely in the realm of understanding, but also emerge "in act definition where acts can be defined diametrically according to circumstance and perceiver. The result is that every event or act can be defined as good, bad, or neutral, depending upon the frame of reference; the reality of an act is in its realization." The frame of reference, or ethical standard, then, is central to determinations of character and motivation. "There are no absolutely and universally unethical acts; there are only unethical acts according to a particular standard."[5]

Ethical codes, whether legal, religious, or social, provide a necessary reference through which individuals may evaluate their own and others' behavior. While codes vary in the degree of guidance they offer, Crable notes that an ethical code "functions to remove a contention of unethical behavior from the realm of vaguely guided accusation and to place it in the category of clearly argued claim. The code allows a political constituency to accuse a rhetor of misconduct in terms of some particular guideline."[6] In other words, a rhetor may use an ethical code and other explicit standards to legitimize an accusation.

Legitimacy is concerned with evaluation of acts in relation to some set of accepted moral, social, or legal boundaries. Legitimate acts fall within the area sanctioned by consensual standards, and illegitimate acts fall outside those guidelines. Accusations often are made against individuals without reference to any standard. For a charge to be accepted as legitimate, however, the accusation must make the standards and criteria for judgment explicit. A sense of fairness and justice demand that the accuser state "on what grounds" an individual is being charged with unacceptable acts.[7]

Nichols, then, faced three primary rhetorical requirements in reopening Oppenheimer's record to evaluation. First, he had to clearly identify those acts or role enactments that raised questions about Oppenheimer's ability to serve the government. He had to describe the relevant facts of the case.

Second, to make the charges against Oppenheimer legitimate, he had to identify the standards that raised questions about Oppenheimer's continued government service and through which the facts ultimately would be judged.

Third, through his combination of facts and standards, Nichols had to establish that the investigation in 1954 was different from the previous evaluations of Oppenheimer's behavior in 1943 and 1947. Without new facts, new standards, or new combinations of the two, the AEC's renewed interest in Oppenheimer's ability to serve his government would fall outside its stated concern for the national security.

NICHOLS SETS THE STAGE

Nichols began his letter with an affirmation of the AEC authority and standards that allowed the accusations:

Section 10 of the Atomic Energy Act of 1946 places upon the Atomic Energy Commission the responsibility for assuring that individuals are employed by the Commission only when such employment will not endanger the common defense and security. In addition, Executive Order 10450 of April 27, 1953, requires the suspension of employment of any individual where there exists information indicating that his employment may not be clearly consistent with the interests of the national security.[8]

Nichols immediately drew attention not only to the AEC's authority but to new responsibility given to the AEC in 1953. Nichols began the creation of a new case against Oppenheimer by highlighting additional regulations that were relevant to the case. He extends the strategy by suggesting that his letter results from additional (and therefore new) investigation:

As a result of additional investigations as to your character, associations, and loyalty, and review of our personnel security file in the light of the requirements of the Atomic Energy Act and the requirements of Executive Order 10450, there has developed considerable question whether your continued employment on Atomic Energy Commission work will endanger the common defense and security and whether such continued employment is clearly consistent with the interests of the national security.[9]

Nichols's opening paragraphs explained the reasons for and policies behind his letter. These first paragraphs, however, hold much more than a simple explanation and justification. Rhetorically, they typify Burke's "watershed moment."

In these first few words, Nichols raised the central questions that opened Oppenheimer's life to public scrutiny and specifically guided the remainder of his accusations. He framed the case's preeminent question, the "unknown" that required resolution, as, "Is Oppenheimer's continued employment consistent with national security?" The question placed Oppenheimer's employment on one side of an equational scale and national security on the other. The accusation was thus polarized. It required Oppenheimer's judges either to find his employment consistent with national security or to divide him from that arena. In other words, Oppenheimer and his judges were asked to support one of two equations:

$$(\text{Oppenheimer's employment}) = (\text{security})$$

or

$$(\text{Oppenheimer's employment}) \neq (\text{security})$$

Oppenheimer, of course, would argue for the first, positive equation. The judges' eventual choices, however, would depend on the content and value accorded to Oppenheimer's service. If Oppenheimer's employment received a negative value, as Nichols suggests, his employment would not support the positive value of national security.

Since the issue in question was Oppenheimer's security value, Oppenheimer's employment at the initiation of the hearing held an unknown status. No standard of "secure until proven a security risk" was to protect Oppenheimer; he held no legal "presumption of clearance." In fact, the opposite was true: until Oppenheimer disproved the charges, he would not be allowed to serve the government. Although two previous reviews had resulted in Oppenheimer's continued employment, Nichols's letter officially called Oppenheimer to account for twenty years of his life. In algebraic terms, Nichols's letter converted a positive equation into a question. Nichols represented Oppenheimer's relationship to government as:

(Oppenheimer's employment) ? (national security)

The hearing's purpose, then, was to determine whether Oppenheimer's employment was consistent or inconsistent with national security. Oppenheimer would be found "equal to" or "not equal to" the test.

In order to make the security decision, the composition and value of several ambiguous terms required investigation. "Oppenheimer's employment" and "security" and their clusters needed detailed explication and careful consideration. These "clarifications" are the heart of rhetoric's influence. The interpretations and evaluations asserted and defended would not only characterize Oppenheimer's previous service, but would determine the direction of his future relationship with the government, the scientific community, and the public.

NICHOLS DETAILS THE REQUIREMENTS OF SECURITY

The Atomic Energy Act of 1946 states:

No arrangement shall be made (for an individual's employment) . . . until the Federal Bureau of Investigation shall have made an investigation and report to the Commission on the character, associations, and loyalty of such individual and the Commission shall have determined that permitting such person to have access to restricted data will not endanger the common defense or security.[10]

The terms "character," "associations," and "loyalty" are used again in the act's next subsection and, most importantly, are also adopted in Nichols's opening remarks. The terms are emergent evaluative categories that suggest that Oppenheimer's security value is derived from the combined estimation of his character, associations, and loyalty. The terminological equation that results is:

Oppenheimer's employment = character + associations + loyalty

These three compositional terms did not assess Oppenheimer's work directly, but rather called for a definition of Oppenheimer himself. The documents, and the accusations that emerged from them, investigated not Oppenheimer's worth as an advisor per se, but his values as a person. Therefore, the security equations assume that

Oppenheimer, the man = Oppenheimer, the advisor

His personal and professional identities are at least equal, with his personal attributes potentially taking precedence over his professional contributions. As a result, Nichols' question is modified and reduced to:

$$\text{Oppenheimer} = \text{character} + \text{associations} + \text{loyalty}$$

Through substitution, the question at hand is: Are Oppenheimer's character, associations, and loyalty consistent with national security? Rhetorically, Nichols's amplified equation explored Oppenheimer's substance, his identity rather than his actions.

Substance, as Kenneth Burke uses the term, is more than what comprises a person's physical makeup. It is literally a sub-stance, that which "stands beneath or supports the person or thing."[11] Substance is a term of placement. Burke notes that "this idea of locating, or placing, is implicit in our very word for definition itself: to define or determine a thing, is to mark its boundaries."[12] The goal of Nichols, Oppenheimer, and eventually Oppenheimer's judges was to define Oppenheimer and his security-worth, to mark the boundaries of his behavior, and then to compare those boundaries to the definition of "security." Literally, the hearing's purpose was to see if Oppenheimer "measured up." One way to substantiate boundaries, "to tell what a thing is," Burke explains, is to place the thing in "terms of something else."[13] The Atomic Energy Act defined Oppenheimer, or any employee for that matter, in terms of character, associations, and loyalty. In Burkean terms, "character" calls for investigation into directional substance. "Associations" and "loyalty" question familial substance.

Directional substance involves what Burke calls a person's "motivating essence."[14] It locates motives and explanations for action in an individual's internal characteristics. Directional substance asks not " 'who are you?' or 'where are you?' but 'where are you going?' "[15] Since the primary task of the Oppenheimer case was to predict the quality of Oppenheimer's future actions and decisions, directional substance was a central concern. His actions would be explored for the purposes they served.

People also look to an individual's past for principles and beliefs that guide action, in order to make predictions about future action. Familial substance turns attention from a person's internal motivations to motives that arise from an individual's "ancestry," or group memberships. As Brummett explains, "this method will describe a person's motivations and actions as arising because of his/her class, social group, nationality, and affiliations."[16] The terms "associations" and "loyalty" ask for such a description. A concern for a person's social roles is closely tied to familial substance.

Even these terms, which are more specific than "Oppenheimer, the person," are ambiguous and provide further opportunity for transformation and redefinition. While Oppenheimer would use this resource in his defense, the accusation tried to lessen interpretive ambiguity with reference to more concrete standards. The explicit directives of Executive Order

10450 eliminated some of the equivocalities found in Nichols's equation and supposedly insured a more "secure" decision by the authorities.

Executive Order 10450, sometimes called Eisenhower's security program, provided for investigation of all civil servants. Enacted in early 1953, the order's suggested investigative categories responded to rampant paranoia over the communist threat. Some of the categories were:

(i) Any behavior, activities, or associations which tend to show that the individual is not reliable or trustworthy.

(ii) Any deliberate misrepresentations, falsifications, or omission of material facts.

(v) Any facts which furnish reason to believe that the individual may be subjected to coercion, influence, or pressure which may cause him to act contrary to the best interests of the national security.

(5) Membership in, or affiliation or sympathetic association with, any foreign or domestic organization, association, movement, group, or combination of persons which is totalitarian, Fascist, Communist, or subversive, or which has adopted or shows, a policy of advocating or approving the commission of acts of force or violence to deny other persons ther rights under the constitution of the United States or which seeks to alter the form of government of the United States by unconstitutional means.[17]

Each category presents a condition that, if it pertains to the case in question, outweighs any positive factors in the balance. These criteria list behaviors or personal characteristics inconsistent with security, so that:

$$(+\text{security}) \neq (-\text{untrustworthiness})$$

$$(+\text{security}) \neq (-\text{deliberate misrepresentations})$$

$$(+\text{security}) \neq (-\text{susceptibility to coercion or influence})$$

$$(+\text{security}) \neq (-\text{associations with subversive groups})$$

While only the fourth is linked specifically to the overall equation by the term "associations," the first three categories might be considered relevant to estimations of character. If a person is described by any or all of the criteria, then at least one compository security term is presumed negative.

Yet another AEC document relevant to the case, "Criteria for Determining Eligibility for Security Clearance of November, 1950," reiterated the negative weights assigned by these criteria.[18] The 1950 document calls these investigative areas "types of derogatory information." The term "derogatory" furthers the negative values associated with the described behaviors or characteristics. These standards, then, give a reference point for security value weights.

Note that although Nichols referred to the Atomic Energy Act and to Executive Order 10450 and included copies of both documents with his letter, he failed to outline the specific document subsections that were relevant to his accusations or to specifically explain his interpretation of the documents. Despite his apparent assumption that the documents were clear and exhaustive, his charges reveal more than the documents do about the clarity and unambiguous nature of the "negative" criteria.

NICHOLS SPECIFIES THE CHARGES

With the major equations and evaluative standards exposed, Nichols presented "the substance of the information which raised the question concerning Oppenheimer's eligibility for employment on Atomic Energy Commission work." Nichols began to tie the "facts" of the case to the standards of judgment. He began with an exploration of the security equation term "associations."

Associations

Nichols began with a lengthy list of Oppenheimer's past associations in the list, the term with perhaps the greatest significance and value weight in Nichols's terminology, "communist," appeared forty-two times. The first piece of derogatory information Nichols presented is typical of his charges:

It was reported that in 1940 you were listed as a sponsor of the Friends of the Chinese People, an organization which was characterized in 1944 by the House Committee on Un-American Activities as a Communist-front organization.[19]

Nichols explicitly identified Oppenheimer with three other communist organizations and noted his relationships with known communists. Along with Oppenheimer's formal and informal contact with Communist party members was the fact that his brother, his sister-in-law, his wife, and a former fiancée had all joined the Communist party at some time.[20]

Nichols spoke of communism with obvious negativity, in accordance with the government's definition. He tied Oppenheimer's past associations directly to the security standard at work in the case.

The Communist party has been designated by the Attorney General as a subversive organization which seeks to alter the form of government of the United States by unconstitutional means, within the purview of Executive Order 9835 and Executive Order 10450.[21]

From these first charges, several definitive and evaluative equations emerged. First, communism was assigned a negative weight based on its composition. Communists were subversive, unconstitutional, and by implication un-American. Only a completely negative representation was accurate:

$$(-\text{communism}) = (-\text{subversive}) + (-\text{unconstitutional}) + (-\text{un-American})$$

Notice that each term defines the negative of another term—sub-versive, unconstitutional, un-American. By connecting Oppenheimer with Communists, Nichols made at least one term in his overall security equation, "associations," negative. Through substitution, one term in the equation becomes "known":

$$(?\text{Oppenheimer}) \ ? \ (?\text{character}) + (-\text{communist associations}) + (?\text{loyalty})$$

Character

Nichols used several strategies to call Oppenheimer's character into question. He attempted to point out numerous contradictions between Oppenheimer's actions and his words and to establish that Oppenheimer had lied to security officials on at least one occasion.

Nichols carried the communist question beyond mere association into matters of policy. He pointed to Oppenheimer's statement that he supported a "no hiring policy" for Communists at Los Alamos, and then suggested that, despite his statements to the contrary, Oppenheimer had indeed supported employment of Communists in classified work.

You state in August of 1943 that you did not want anybody working for you on the Project who was a member of the Communist party, since "one always had a question of divided loyalty." . . . It was also reported that during the period 1942-45 you were responsible for the employment on the atom bomb project of individuals who were members of the Communist party.[22]

This charge gave explicit attention to what may be considered inconsistencies, contradictions, or even lies in Oppenheimer's record. A similar theme appeared earlier in Nichols's letter:

It was further reported that you attended a closed meeting of the professional section of the Communist Party . . . at your residence. . . . It was further reported that you denied that you attended such a meeting and that such a meeting was held in your home.[23]

In both cases, Nichols cast doubt on Oppenheimer's candor and veracity.

In addition to the negative tone of these charges, the Chevalier Incident, the most damaging evidence of Oppenheimer's questionable integrity, figured prominently not only in Nichols's charges but also in all other case documents. The Chevalier Incident must be explained before analysis of the case may proceed.

In January or February 1943, Oppenheimer's close personal friend Haakon Chevalier approached him at a dinner party to tell him that George C. Eltenton, another Berkeley professor, had a means to pass technical information to the Russians. Oppenheimer then flatly stated that he would have no part in such a transaction, but he waited nearly eight months before he reported the incident to an Army intelligence officer, Colonel Boris T. Pash, on 26 August 1943. At that time, Oppenheimer said that three people had been approached by Eltenton's intermediary, but he refused to name Chevalier as the go-between. On 12 September 1943, Oppenheimer was again interrogated about the incident, this time by a Colonel John Landsdale, Jr. Again Oppenheimer refused to name Chevalier, saying, "it is a question of some past loyalties."[24] Finally, in December 1943, Oppenheimer revealed Chevalier's connection to General Groves, the commanding officer of the Los Alamos project. Later in 1946, the FBI questioned Oppenheimer about the Chevalier Incident, at which time he admitted that his story to Colonels Pash and Landsdale concerning three scientists was a fabrication.

In light of these charges, Oppenheimer's character also appeared suspect. While these accusations are perhaps less explicitly negative than those concerned with associations, Nichols portrayed Oppenheimer's character as unreliable, at the very least. The overall equation records Nichols's indications as:

$$(-\text{Oppenheimer's record}) = (-\text{faithfulness to security procedures})$$

The Chevalier incident not only shifted the character evaluation to the negative, but also raised doubt about Oppenheimer's loyalty.

Loyalty

While in Nichols's terminology loyalty generally required faithfulness to U.S. interests, Oppenheimer's role as a scientific advisor to the government created additional requirements, beyond those of an average citizen. It demanded loyalty to the security system and to the organizational hierarchy. Oppenheimer's fidelity, Nichols argued, was questionable in both areas.

Oppenheimer took great license with the security system when he hired known Communists. From Nichols's point of view, in the Chevalier Incident, Oppenheimer failed to report an espionage attempt. In both cases Oppenheimer apparently felt it proper to disregard the security procedures that governed his employment. He followed his personal analysis of the situation rather than those procedures. For Nichols, these decisions raised questions about Oppenheimer's loyalty.

The most controversial charge against Oppenheimer was that of disloyalty. Nichols suggested that Oppenheimer had slowed the development of the hydrogen bomb after President Truman called for a crash program.

Since that lack of enthusiasm threatened the national security, according to Nichols, Oppenheimer was disloyal, this time to the administration's goals.

Nichols first summarized Oppenheimer's recommendations about the hydrogen bomb as follows:

It was reported that in 1945 you expressed the view that "there is a reasonable possibility that it [the hydrogen bomb] can be made," but that the feasibility of the hydrogen bomb did not appear, on theoretical grounds, as certain as the fission bomb appeared certain, on theoretical grounds, when the Los Alamos Laboratory was started.

Oppenheimer was hardly alone in this view, and the Los Alamos project bore out his evaluation of the situation. Oppenheimer's later recommendations, given the luxury of hindsight, could be challenged further by Nichols.

[It was reported] that in the autumn of 1949, the General Advisory Committee expressed the view that "an imaginative and concerted attack on the problem has a better than even chance of producing the weapon within 5 years."[25]

Nichols established Oppenheimer's belief that the hydrogen bomb was theoretically possible. He then moves to a second phase of the accusation:

It was further reported that in the autumn of 1949, and subsequently, you strongly opposed the development of the hydrogen bomb; (1) on moral grounds, (2) by claiming that it was not feasible, (3) by claiming that there were insufficient facilities and scientific personnel to carry on the development, and (4) that it was not politically desirable.[26]

The Nichols characterization of Oppenheimer's record on the hydrogen bomb builds in negativity. He then charged that Oppenheimer actively opposed the hydrogen bomb program:

It was further reported that even after it was determined, as a matter of national policy, to proceed with development of a hydrogen bomb, you continued to oppose the project and declined to cooperate fully in the project.[27]

Nichols implied that, prior to the president's decision, open discussion and even advocacy would have been appropriate. But once the decision was made to go ahead with the Superbomb, anything but "full cooperation" violated Oppenheimer's advisory role. Nichols listed specific cases that raised concern:

It was further reported that you departed from your proper role as an adviser to the Commission by causing the distribution separately and in private, to top personnel at Los Alamos of the majority and minority reports of the General Advisory Committee on development of the hydrogen bomb for the purpose of trying to turn such top personnel against the development of the hydrogen bomb. It was further reported that you were instrumental in persuading other outstanding scientists not to work on the hydrogen bomb project.[28]

Nichols clearly noted that any active opposition to the project violated Oppenheimer's "advisory role." To this point, the H-bomb issue raised questions about Oppenheimer's "loyalty" to the procedures and requirements of the security system. However, Nichols's final paragraph evaluated Oppenheimer's actions according to their results:

The opposition to the hydrogen bomb of which you are the most experienced, most powerful and most effective member, has definitely slowed down its development.[29]

This description can be recast as a challenge to Oppenheimer's organizational loyalty through the following equations. If:

$$\text{loyalty} = \text{loyalty to the nation} + \text{loyalty to security regulations} + \text{loyalty to presidential administration}$$

then:

$$(?\text{Oppenheimer}) ? (-\text{character}) + (-\text{communist associations}) + (-\text{loyalties})$$

SECURITY SUM

Nichols fitted these pieces of derogatory information into the overall security equation with this summary:

In view of your access to highly sensitive classified information, and in view of these allegations which, until disproved, raise questions as to your veracity, conduct and even your loyalty, the commission has no other recourse, in the discharge of its obligations to protect the common defense and security, but to suspend your clearance until the matter has been resolved.[30]

The terms "veracity" and "conduct" may be considered compository terms for "character." Both what a person says and what a person does, and the consistency between words and actions, reflect that person's character. These compository terms further illustrate Nichols's negative evaluation of Oppenheimer's character. The Chevalier Incident, in particular, suggested that neither Oppenheimer's veracity nor his conduct was above challenge.

Nichols's summary also implied a hierarchy of "character," "associations," and "loyalty," in which loyalty is given a special significance or value. The phrase "and even your loyalty" may suggest that a charge of "disloyalty" is the most serious possible accusation. It also might indicate that while Oppenheimer's acts had been questioned before, in this instance further investigation challenged even his previously unquestioned loyalty. In Nichols's terminology, therefore:

$$\text{loyalty} > \text{character} + \text{associations}$$

While "loyalty" is never defined or connected explicitly to any particular charge, an overall reading of Nichols's accusations reveals a subtle undercurrent that at least raises doubt about Oppenheimer's loyalty to his role within government and to the country in general.

In summary, Nichols's accusations can be represented by a series of equations that incorporate specific standards and behaviors within a broad definition of security. The most clearly defined aspect of these accusations is the negative value assigned to Oppenheimer's communist associations. The least well-defined term is "loyalty," despite Nichols's suggestion that loyalty may hold overriding significance. Algebraically, the accusations can be encapsulated in these equations:

$$(+\text{security}) \ ? \ (?\text{Oppenheimer})$$

$$(+\text{security}) \ ? \ (?\text{character}) + (?\text{associations}) + (?\text{loyalty})$$

$$(+\text{security}) \ ? \ (-\text{character}) + (-\text{communist associations}) + (-\text{loyalty})$$

$$(+\text{security}) \ ? \ [(-\text{veracity}) + (-\text{conduct})] + (-\text{communist associations}) + (-\text{LOYALTY})$$

Nichols framed the discussion for the hearing within these general equations. He linked communist associations, veracity, conduct, and loyalty with the decision to be made—the determination of Oppenheimer's status as a security risk. It is within that terminological frame that Oppenheimer answered the charges.

OPPENHEIMER REPLIES

Oppenheimer, along with his counsel Lloyd Garrison, responded to Nichols's charges with what Garrison called a "whole man approach."

We felt there was no way of arriving at a final conclusion about whether this fellow should be entrusted with atomic secrets or not other than the combined judgment of men of the highest integrity and reputation of what they felt about him. This seemed to us much more conclusive than the dredging up of all these little incidents from his past which in the extraordinary atmosphere of the time were magnified in importance . . . a hundred fold.[31]

In accord with the whole man approach, Oppenheimer replied to the charges with an autobiographical letter that served as the major defense document. Oppenheimer wrote, "I cannot ignore the question you have raised nor accept the suggestion that I am unfit for public service. The items of so-called 'derogatory information' set forth in your letter cannot be fairly understood except in the context of my life and work."[32]

Whether or not Oppenheimer realized the rhetorical implications of his statement, he indicated the importance of terminological context and the evolution of terms. The temporal context in which terms are placed may change the terms' meanings significantly. For instance, in Oppenheimer's view the term "communist" carried vastly different implications in 1954 than it had before 1945. The term had undergone a transformation that increased in negativity as the Soviet Union emerged as a post–World War II adversary. Garrison feared the result of decontextualized terms. He noted that "given the then temper of the times, there was a grave danger that particular items in the catalogue of the Commission's charges would be wrested out of context and judged in isolation without regard to the time when they occurred."[33]

Oppenheimer's strategy, then, emphasized contextual substance as well as the directional and familiar substance explored by Nichols. Contextual substance defines a person in terms of a "scene, environment, situation, context, ground."[34] This definitional method suggests that motives should be interpreted, to some degree, as arising from surroundings. Oppenheimer defined his actions within the many and varied roles he had played throughout his life. Oppenheimer's challenge was to cluster the terms and their situational stimuli into temporal and role-related contexts in such a way as to support a positive sum in the security equation. He accepted Nichols's overall equation

$$security = character + associations + loyalty$$

but disputed the definitional methods used and the values assigned to the terms that figured into his "security sum."

Oppenheimer's whole-man contextual strategy depended on the judge's acceptance of the proposition that people, like the terms that describe them, change. By supplying a strictly chronological autobiography, Oppenheimer was able to show his development over more than twenty years. He presented an equational progression which, he hoped, would capture his political evolution and establish his 1954 "security sum" as positive and consistent with security.

Oppenheimer Begins: The Eccentric Scholar

In the opening pages of Oppenheimer's reply, he described himself as a devoted teacher and scholar, "almost wholly divorced from the contempo-

rary scene in this country."[35] Oppenheimer's separation from public life
was unusually extreme.

I never read a newspaper or a current magazine like *Time* or *Harper's*; I had no
radio, no telephone; I learned of the stock market crash in the fall of 1929 only long
after the event; the first time I ever voted was in the Presidential election of 1936.[36]

Oppenheimer admitted that his friends, who were university faculty, scientists, classicists, and artists, had chided him about his somewhat bizarre
seclusion. Most important to his defense, however, was that this behavior,
no matter how aberrant, clearly was not political. Oppenheimer presented
his pre-1936 autobiographical summary as:

$$pre\text{-}1936 \text{ Oppenheimer} = teacher + scholar + friend$$

If this definitional equation were translated into Nichols's overall equation,
Oppenheimer, while not interested in government, was no threat to security
either. His 1936 security sum would be positive:

$$+pre\text{-}1936 \text{ Oppenheimer} = (+character) + (+associations) + (+loyalty)$$

Oppenheimer then reported the first major shift in his political interests,
his first "awakening." He wrote that "these changes did not alter my
earlier friendships, my relations to my physics; but they added something
new."[37] The "something new" was a political interest. Oppenheimer did
not eliminate the extant equational terms; he merely expanded the
equation's scope to include politics.

He credited the shift in his political interest to a growing awareness of
German anti-Semitism and of the effect of the Great Depression upon his
students. He wrote that, through his students, he "began to understand
how deeply political and economic events could affect men's lives. I began
to feel the need to participate more fully in the life of community. But I had
no framework of political conviction or experience to give me perspective in
these matters."[38] Oppenheimer added a political interest to his equation and
concurrently suggested the nature of that interest. He suggested that he had
progressed from political reclusiveness to political naïveté. The progression
is represented in Figure 4.1.

Oppenheimer Evolves: The Political Activist

After 1936, Oppenheimer did associate with known Communists. His
growing involvement with communist organizations prompted Nichols
to degrade Oppenheimer's associational value. Neither Oppenheimer's
veracity nor his conduct were flawless in terms of security; Oppenheimer

Figure 4.1
Oppenheimer's 1936 Progression

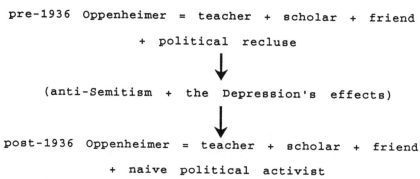

could not deny his known activities. However, he did attempt to counteract the negative connotations evoked by Nichols's descriptions of those activities and associations.

First, he tried to characterize his associations as motivated less by strong political opinions than by a search for political identity. He wrote that he had "liked the new sense of companionship, and at the same time felt that I was coming to be part of the life of my time and country."[39] Moreover, he described the period as one in which Communists "joined with non-Communist groups in support of humanitarian objectives."[40] His sympathy with one "humanitarian objective," the Spanish Loyalist cause, he admitted was "not a matter of understanding and informed convictions."[41] He said, "Like a great many other Americans I was emotionally committed to the Loyalist cause."[42] Despite his admissions of communist associations and his monetary support of left-wing organizations, Oppenheimer denied an explicitly political connection to communism. He stated, "I never was a member of the Communist party. I never accepted communist dogma or theory; in fact, it never made sense to me. I had no clearly formulated political views. I hated tyranny and repression and every form of dictatorial control of thought."[43]

From these descriptions, Oppenheimer rounded out the term "associations" as admittedly political and communist, but also as naïve and motivated by a sincere wish to fight tyranny, rather than by communist ideology. Beyond that, the ideology he did espouse was general and hardly sinister. Oppenheimer did not challenge the label "communist" so much as he objected to the significance attached to that label in retrospect. He suggested that late-1930s communism was not the evil threat perceived in 1954. The weight and value Oppenheimer assigned to his communist associations neither supported nor degraded his security sum. He felt that his associations had been insignificant. For him, communism in the late 1930s had been an outlet for a desire to participate in politics and nothing more threatening than a personal adventure into a new area. He presented his past activities as irrelevant to the questions at hand. While both "communism" and therefore "associations" were both significant and negative in Nichols's terminology, Oppenheimer asserted that no threat existed in his associations, no matter what their ethical value.

Moreover, Oppenheimer felt that "loyalty" outweighed "associations." His good intentions, in his view, changed the entire picture. At the hearing, Oppenheimer's attorney supported this hierarchy in his closing remarks.

In trying to reach your determination you have some guides. . . . The statute speaks of character, associations, and loyalty. Certainly loyalty is the paramount consideration. If a man is loyal, if in his heart he loves his country and would not knowingly or willingly do anything to injure its security, the associations and character become relatively unimportant.[44]

Oppenheimer reinforced Nichols's hierarchy in explicit terms. He too emphasized loyalty and asserted that it outweighed all other factors relevant to his "security sum":

$$(\text{post-1936 Oppenheimer}) = (+\text{character}) + (-\text{communist associations}) + (+\text{LOYALTY})$$

For Oppenheimer, however, "loyalty" is measured by intentions, not ultimate results of action.

Despite his emphasis on loyalty, Oppenheimer apparently felt that an explanation of his motives was insufficient to nullify Nichols's negative assertions concerned with communism. Accordingly, Oppenheimer also tried to overcome any assumed connection between assocations and loyalty.

In his description of Jean Tatlock, a communist and his former fiancée, Oppenheimer wrote that "she loved this country and its people and its life."[45] Oppenheimer described his wife, a former Communist party member, as a person of "whose integrity and loyalty to the United States I had no question." Although communists, both women were loyal to the United States. If the relationship between these communists and loyalty is generalized, Oppenheimer implicitly challenges Nichols's assumption that

$$(-\text{communism}) \neq (+\text{loyalty})$$

Beyond individual cases, Oppenheimer tried to go beyond the mere title "communist" to the purposes of specific organizations. Nichols had merely named organizations as communist fronts and assumed that this description alone proved their negative value. Oppenheimer, on the other hand, described the groups' positive goals. He depicted the Consumer's Union, one of Nichols's communist-front organizations, as a group "concerned with evaluating information on products of interest."[46] The American Committee for Democracy and Intellectual Freedom, in Oppenheimer's terms, "stood as a protest against what happened to intellectuals and professionals in Germany."[47] When described with Oppenheimer's terminology, when *placed in context*, these "communists" may be equated with freedom and positive political involvement.

After reading Oppenheimer's descriptions, Nichols's negative evaluation of Oppenheimer's associations seems less significant, if not less negative, in Oppenheimer's security sum. Moreover, Oppenheimer's terminology, like Nichols's terminology, reveals a hierarchy in which "loyalty" outweighs the other definitional terms. Oppenheimer spent much of his explanation showing that, no matter his associations, he had always had noble, loyal motives. Oppenheimer apparently believed that his professed loyalty outweighed his association problems, so that even if his associations were valued negatively by the judges, as Nichols proposed, Oppenheimer's security sum would still be positive, as shown in this equation:

$$(+ \text{post-1936 Oppenheimer} = (+ \text{character}) + (- \text{communist associations}) + (+ \text{LOYALTY})$$

Once Oppenheimer had described his communist associations, he began to signal a second political progression with temporal terms. For instance, he said, "I did not then [1936] regard Communists as dangerous; and some of their declared objectives seemed to me desirable."[48] His use of "then" implied a changed view at some future time. This second shift had lasted over several years and primarily involved a changed view of Russia.

Oppenheimer came to see the Soviet Union as "a land of purge and terror, of ludicrously bad management and of a long-suffering people."[49] He again used temporal terms to signal a shift—"*at that time* I did not fully understand—*as in time* I came to understand—how completely the Communist party in this country was under the control of Russia. . . . I found myself increasingly out of sympathy with the policy of disengagement and neutrality that the Communist Press advocated" (emphasis added).[50] The shift was complete by 1943, when Oppenheimer's energy was needed in the war effort. "By the time that we moved to Los Alamos in early 1943, both as a result of my changed views and of the great pressure of war work, my participation in left-wing organizations and my associations with left-wing circles had ceased and were never to be reestablished."[51]

Oppenheimer had finally adopted the negative, "mainstream" view of communism. After 1943, he assigned a negative value to American communism, thus:

$$(- \text{communism}) \neq (+ \text{security})$$

By this point in his reply, Oppenheimer had answered most of Nichols's charges related to communism. Oppenheimer's equations suggested that, even given the worst view of communism, he had weathered his life's most turbulent period and emerged a "secure" government employee. His troublesome communist associations were removed from the equation, while the positive values assigned to character and loyalty remained, as shown in Figure 4.2.

Figure 4.2
Oppenheimer's 1943 Progression

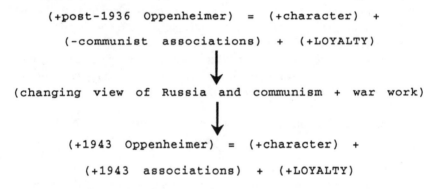

```
(+post-1936 Oppenheimer) = (+character) +

  (-communist associations) + (+LOYALTY)
                         │
                         ▼
(changing view of Russia and communism + war work)
                         │
                         ▼
     (+1943 Oppenheimer) = (+character) +

       (+1943 associations) + (+LOYALTY)
```

Oppenheimer Serves: The Scientific Advisor

After Oppenheimer described his second political awakening, only three major allegations remained unanswered: (1) that he had hired known Communists at Los Alamos, (2) that he had failed to report Chevalier's supposed espionage attempt, and (3) that he had opposed hydrogen bomb development inappropriately. In keeping with his "whole man" strategy, Oppenheimer situated each charge within his life and work.

The charges regarding Communists employed at Los Alamos and the Chevalier Incident related Oppenheimer's years as director of the Los Alamos project. He described the period as one filled with problems. Wartime recruiting had been difficult, but Oppenheimer explained that a sense of patriotism and duty outweighed the scientists' misgivings.

The notion of disappearing into the New Mexico desert for an indeterminate period and under quasi-military auspices disturbed a good many scientists. . . . But there was another side to it. Almost everyone knew that it was an unparalleled opportunity to bring to bear the basic knowledge and art of science for the benefit of his country. Almost everyone knew that his job, if it were achieved, would be a part of history. This sense of excitement, of devotion and of patriotism in the end prevailed.[52]

At Los Alamos, patriotism and devotion had outweighed all hardships. Oppenheimer connected the "Los Alamos loyalty" to the project's leader, himself; as such, it thereby further supported the positive values assigned to loyalty in his security equation.

This loyalty issue, critical to Oppenheimer's terminology, again was linked to communism at Los Alamos. Nichols reported that while Oppenheimer had said he did not approve of employment of Communists at Los Alamos, he had nevertheless been instrumental in hiring Communists into the project. Oppenheimer used the urgent context of Los Alamos and the separation of associations and loyalty already argued to counter the apparent contradiction in his record:

We had information in those days of German activity in the field of nuclear fission. We were aware of what it might mean if they beat us to the draw in the development of atomic bombs. The consensus of all our opinions, and every directive that I had, stressed the extreme urgency of our work, as well as the need for guarding all knowledge of it from our enemies. Past Communist connections or sympathies did not necessarily disqualify a man from employment, if we had confidence in his integrity and dependability as a man.[53]

Again Oppenheimer's terminology dissociates character and loyalty from associations:

$$\text{character} + \text{loyalty} > \text{associations}$$

$$\text{integrity} + \text{dependability} > -\text{past communist associations}$$

Note that current communist associations are not addressed specifically. The loyalty/association inequality deals only with *past* communist associations. The inequality also reinforces Oppenheimer's earlier contention that a person's character and loyalty may outweigh any negative implications carried by previous associations. Moreover, if this explanation was acceptable within the Los Alamos context, it might also be deemed reasonable in Oppenheimer's 1954 circumstances.

Oppenheimer used the employment of Communists allegation to answer questions about his loyalty to security procedures and to the administration. When he discussed a request of transfer for a purported Communist, Oppenheimer pointed out that "this request, like all others, was subject to the assumption that the usual security requirements would apply; and when I was told that there was objection on security grounds to this transfer, I was much surprised, but of course agreed."[54] Oppenheimer thus stated that he had subordinated his personal judgment to security proceedings, so that the following equation guided his actions:

$$\text{security system} > \text{personal judgment}$$

Oppenheimer asserted that his loyalty to the security system was positive, therefore:

$$(+LOYALTY) = (+loyalty\ to\ country) + (+loyalty\ to\ security\ system)$$

If "personal judgment" is placed in the equation, it must have lesser significance, as shown here:

$$(+LOYALTY) = (LOYALTY\ TO\ COUNTRY) + (LOYALTY\ TO\ SECURITY\ SYSTEM) + (loyalty\ to\ personal\ judgments)$$

The relationship between the security system and personal judgment is central to Oppenheimer's explanation of the Chevalier Incident. He first recounted his interpretation of his incriminating exchange with Chevalier. He then framed his response to the incident as one supported by good, but misguided, motives:

Nothing in our long-standing friendship would have led me to believe that Chevalier was actually seeking information, and I was certain that he had no idea of the work on which I was engaged. It has long been clear to me that I should have reported the incident at once. . . . I still think of Chevalier as a friend.[55]

Here Oppenheimer adopted a repentant posture and reaffirmed the security system's priority over his own personal judgment.

In the next paragraph Oppenheimer again turned his attention to the Los Alamos scientists' patriotic devotion and, for the first time in the letter, took some credit for their success.

Los Alamos was a remarkable community, inspired by a high sense of mission, of duty and of destiny, coherent, dedicated, and remarkably selfless. . . . These years of hard and loyal work of the scientists culminated in the test on July 16, 1945. It was a success. . . . At the time, it was hard for me not to accept the conclusion that I had managed the enterprise well and played a key part in its success.[56]

Oppenheimer was subtly reminding his judges that after 1945 he had assumed the role of "father of the atomic bomb." Although he humbly asserted that Los Alamos "was the very opposite of a one-man show,"[57] at the same time, the document showed that the accused was no small figure in World War II history. And as Oppenheimer's chronology continued, his high status became even more obvious. He had been propelled to a level of influence never before afforded a scientist, as demonstrated in the brief list of his advisory posts during the late 1940s.[58] His equation, expanding in content and in significance, is shown in Figure 4.3.

As Oppenheimer's influence and status grew, he and other scientists had

Figure 4.3
Oppenheimer's 1945 Progression

```
(+1943 Oppenheimer) = (+character) + (+1943 associations)
                    + (+LOYALTY)
```

↓

```
(+1945 Oppenheimer) = (+character) + (+current associations)
 + (+loyalty to country) + (+loyalty to security system)
```

created the new role of scientific advisor. The proper purview of that role
was central to Nichols's question about the hydrogen bomb decision.

Oppenheimer seemed to sense that, to defend his actions after World War
II, it was important to give recognition to a scientist's limited expertise and
limited advisory role. As the introduction to this section, Oppenheimer
offered an explicit statement of his intentions and motives. "I need to turn
now to an account of some of the measures which, as Chairman of the
General Advisory Committee, and in other capacities, I advocated in the
years since the war to increase the power of the United States and its allies to
resist and defeat aggression."[59]

Oppenheimer left no room for doubt about the purposes that guided his
recommendations. He then further defined the scientific advisor's role. He
wrote, "When I and other scientists were called on for advice, our principle
duty was to make our technical experience and judgment available."[60] He
noted the limitations of the GAC scientists, in particular, when he wrote that

formulation of policy and the management of the vast atomic energy enterprise were
responsibilities vested in the commission itself. . . . The General Advisory Committee had the role which was fixed for it by statute, to advise the Commission. In that
capacity we gave the Commission our views on questions which the Commission put
before us, brought to the Commission's attention on our initiative technical matters
of importance, and encouraged and supported the work of the several major instal-
lations of the Commission. . . . It was not our function to formulate military
requirements.[61]

Oppenheimer's statements might be construed as reinforcement or
evidence for his loyalty to the president's administration and executive organization. Having already indicated that he subordinated his personal
judgment to the security system, Oppenheimer also needed to subordinate a
scientist's advice to administrative decisions. Scientists, in Oppenheimer's
terminology, were technical, not military or political, advisors. Moreover, he
was one of a group that advised the government. Oppenheimer reinforces
this move from individual action to group action through a shift from the
first person to the third. He alone did not influence his scientific colleagues.

Additionally, in most cases the committee had complied with commission requests. The scientists were not involved in raising issues or in affirmative advocacy. They offered their opinions, generally, only when such advice was solicited.

In all his previous definitional strategies, Oppenheimer encouraged the judges to place his actions in broader temporal and political contexts. In this case, however, Oppenheimer narrowed the context of his definition. These role limitations were central to Oppenheimer's defense of his role in hydrogen bomb development.

Recall that Nichols argued that Oppenheimer had overstepped the bounds of his advisory role when he espoused political views in recommending against the H-bomb. In both Oppenheimer's terminology and in the government's terminology,

$$\text{scientific advisor} \neq \text{political advisor}$$

Whatever the violation of his proper advisory role, Oppenheimer asserted that the motivations that undergirded the GAC report were loyal.

I think I am correct in asserting that the unanimous opposition we expressed to the crash program was based on the conviction, to which technical considerations as well as others contributed, that because of our over-all situation at that time such a program might weaken rather than strengthen the position of the United States.[62]

Not only did Oppenheimer support the committee's motives in advising against the H-bomb, but he further submitted that he had faithfully followed the executive directive that contradicted the committee's advice.

This is the full story of my "opposition to the hydrogen bomb." . . . It is a story which ended once and for all when in January 1950, the President announced his decision to proceed with the program. I never urged anyone not to work on the hydrogen bomb project. . . . We [the GAC] never again raised the question of the wisdom of the policy which had been settled, but concerned ourselves rather with trying to implement it.[63]

Oppenheimer was aware that the term "loyalty" required his allegiance not only to country and security procedures, but also to the administrative hierarchy of which he was a part. Thus the term "loyalty," in Oppenheimer's terminology, involved these compository terms:

$$\text{loyalty} = \text{loyalty to country} + \text{loyalty to security system}$$
$$+ \text{loyalty to organizational hierarchy}$$

In determining the value of each term that comprised "loyalty," in each case

Oppenheimer stressed both his positive intentions and the demonstration of loyalty presented in his acts.

Oppenheimer made a final attempt to highlight his "positive" efforts for the United States in his closing remarks:

I have had to deal briefly or not at all with instances in which my actions or views were adverse to Soviet or Communist interest, and of actions that testify to my devotion to freedom, or that have contributed to the vitality, influence, and power of the United States.[64]

Oppenheimer asserted that active opposition to communism had often guided his actions. He also referred to more evidence to support a positive valuing of his loyalty to the country. Oppenheimer could only hope that his entire discussion revealed a trustworthy character. His final paragraph pleaded for acceptance of his characterization rather than those of his accusers.

In preparing this letter, I have reviewed two decades of my life. I have recalled instances where I acted unwisely. What I hoped was, not that I could wholly avoid error, but that I might learn from it. What I have learned has, I think, made me more fit to serve my country.[65]

Oppenheimer's reply came full circle, as he again drew attention to change over time and suggested that his security sum was more positive then, in 1954, than at all previous times. Since he had twice before received security clearance, acceptance of his self-description would make him even more worthy of government employment in 1954 than he had been in 1943 or 1947. Oppenheimer's primary proposal, based on his answers to Nichols's charges, and the subsequent positive security sum Oppenheimer advocated, was:

$$+ 1954 \text{ Oppenheimer} > (+ 1943 \text{ Oppenheimer}) + (+ 1947 \text{ Oppenheimer})$$

EMERGENT ISSUES

A comparison of the equations that are presented in Nichols's accusations and Oppenheimer's defense generates several issues relevant to the case's resolution. Figures 4.4 and 4.5 summarize the Nichols and Oppenheimer positions in equations.

First, "character," "associations," and "loyalty" appear as compository terms in both Nichols's and Oppenheimer's security equations. Both Nichols and Oppenheimer gave loyalty special significance in their equations. The standards themselves were not challenged openly, only inter-

Figure 4.4
The Nichols Position

Nichols' Overall Equation

(+security) ? (?Oppenheimer's employment)

(+security) ? (?Oppenheimer)

(+security) ? (?character) + (?association)
+ (?loyalty)

Documented Standards

(+security) ≠ (-untrustworthiness)
(+security) ≠ (-deliberate misrepresentations)
(+security) ≠ (-susceptibility to coercion or
influence)
(+security) ≠ (-associations with subversive
organizations)

Associations

(-communism) = (-subversion) + (-unconstitutional
activity) + (-un-American sentiment)
(-Oppenheimer's associations) = (-communist associations)
(-associations)

Character

(?character) = (?veracity) + (?conduct)
(-veracity) and (-conduct)
(-charcater) = (-veracity) + (-conduct)
(-character)

Loyalty

Loyalty > character + associations
security = character + associations + LOYALTY
(?loyalty)

Nichols' Proposed Security Sum for Oppenheimer

(+security) ≠ (-character) + (-associations)
+ (?LOYALTY)

Figure 4.5
The Oppenheimer Position

<u>Oppenheimer's Overall Equation</u>

(+security)   ?   (?Oppenheimer)

(+security)   ?   (?character) + (?association) + (?loyalty)

(+Oppenheimer)   ?   (?character) + (?associations)
+ (?loyalty)

<u>Oppenheimer's Evolutionary Defense</u>

(+pre-1936 Oppenheimer) = (+character) + (+associations)
+ (+loyalty)

---

pre-Oppenheimer = teacher + scholar + friend
+political recluse
↓
(anti-Semitism + the Depression's effects)
↓
post-1936 Oppenheimer = teacher + scholar +
friend + naive political activist

↓
(+post-1936 Oppenheimer) = (+character) +
(-communist associations) + (+loyalty)
↓
(changed view of Russia + war work)
↓
(+1943 Oppenheimer) = (+character) + (+1943 associations)
+ (+LOYALTY)

(loyalty) = (loyalty to country) + (loyalty to security
system) + (loyalty to organizational hierarchy)
(+loyalty to security system) since security system >
personal judgment

(+loyalty to organizational hierarchy)
since scientific advisor = technical advisor

(+loyalty) = (+loyalty to country) + (loyalty to security
system) + (+loyalty to organizational hierarchy)

(+1954 Oppenheimer) = (+character) + (+association) + (+LOYALTY)

(+1954 Oppenheimer) > (+1943 Oppenheimer) + (1947 Oppenheimer)

<u>Oppenheimer's Proposed Security Sum</u>

(+security) = (+character) + (+association) + (+LOYALTY)

77

preted. The judges were either to adopt this hierarchy or present their own in order to justify their decision.

Second, the definitional methods employed to determine the content and value of character, associations, and loyalty differ significantly in the two terminologies. Nichols emphasized Oppenheimer's apparent purposes and associations without reference to context, and proposed a negative security sum for Oppenheimer. Nichols emphasized the possible negative tendencies in Oppenheimer's background, to point to the direction Oppenheimer was likely to follow in the future. In order to accept Nichols's sum, the judges must agree with his interpretation of documented standards and procedures and their relevance to the substance of his charges. Oppenheimer's strategy, on the other hand, stressed context in order to define his goals and associations as either positive or insignificant. In some cases he simply denied the "facts"; in others, he attempted to diminish the connection between the evaluative standards and his particular acts. He suggested that his past associations could not be fully understood outside the social and political forces of the time. His apparent political direction was meaningful only in the overall context of his scientific advisory role. Oppenheimer's strategy depended on the judges' acceptance of terminological time-embeddedness and evolution. The definitional methods and values chosen greatly influenced the possible case outcomes. The two terminologies offered significantly different orientations toward evaluation of human motive and action.

Third, definitional method also directly affected the value assigned to "communism," a pivotal term in the case. The judges might choose either Nichols's negative estimation of communism or Oppenheimer's positive 1936 evaluation of communism and his negative 1945 reevaluation, or present their own alternative evaluation. The assigned value of communism, whatever it might be, would influence the evaluation of key compository terms.

Fourth, Nichols and Oppenheimer differed over the impact favorable information might have on the security sum. Nichols's charges were all negative, obviously. His interpretation of documented standards submitted that certain acts automatically negate the security sum, no matter what positive contributions are noted. Oppenheimer's primary proposal implied that positive overall contributions might outweigh minor judgmental errors of the past. In accord with his autobiographical strategy, Oppenheimer suggested that if a person learned from past mistakes, those mistakes made that individual better able to serve. Presuming that the person's contributions were positive otherwise, the overall security sum should be positive.

The judges read Nichols's letter, Oppenheimer's reply, all relevant procedural documents, and the FBI and AEC records of Oppenheimer's service and life. After a one-month personnel security hearing, they addressed both Nichols's accusations and Oppenheimer's answers.

NOTES

1. Denise M. Bostdorff summarizes the theories that contribute to this overall in " 'The Decision Is Yours' Campaign: Planned Parenthood's Character-istic Argument of Moral Virtue," in Elizabeth L. Toth and Robert L. Heath, eds., *Rhetorical and Critical Approaches to Public Relations*, 301-13 (Hillsdale, N.J.: Lawrence Erlbaum, 1992).

2. Kenneth Burke, *A Grammar of Motives*, reprint of 1945 edition (Berkeley: University of California Press, 1969), 16.

3. See Bostdorff, " 'Decision Is Yours'," 305. Bostdorff credits Robert C. Elliot for the connection drawn between "person" and "persona." See Robert C. Elliot, *The Literary Persona* (Chicago: University of Chicago Press, 1982), 19.

4. Richard E. Crable, "Ethical Codes, Accountability, and Argumentation," *Quarterly Journal of Speech* 64 (1978): 27.

5. Ibid., 26.

6. Ibid., 27.

7. For a conceptual discussion of legitimacy, see John Dowling and Jeffrey Pfeffer, "Organizational Legitimacy: Social Values and Organizational Behavior," *Pacific Sociological Review* 18 (1975): 122-36.

8. U.S. Atomic Energy Commission, *In the Matter of J. Robert Oppenheimer: Transcript of Hearing before Personnel Security Board* (Washington, D.C.: Government Printing Office, 1954), 3. Hereafter noted as *Transcript*.

9. Ibid.

10. *Congressional Record*, 27 July 1946, 10278.

11. Burke, *Grammar of Motives*, 22.

12. Ibid., 24.

13. Ibid.

14. Ibid., 32.

15. Ibid., 31.

16. Barry Brummett, "Presidential Substance: The Address of August 15, 1973," *Western Journal of Speech Communication* 39 (1975): 252.

17. Executive Order 10450, *Federal Register* 18 (1953): 2491.

18. U.S. Atomic Energy Commission, "Personnel Security Clearance Criteria for Determining Eligibility," *Federal Register* 15 (1950), 8094.

19. *Transcript*, 3.

20. Ibid., 4.

21. Ibid.

22. Ibid., 8.

23. Ibid., 4.

24. Philip M. Stern, *The Oppenheimer Case: Security on Trial* (New York: Harper and Row, 1969), 250.

25. *Transcript*, 6.

26. Ibid.

27. Ibid.

28. Ibid.

29. Ibid.

30. Ibid.

31. Peter Goodchild, *J. Robert Oppenheimer: Shatterer of Worlds* (Boston: Houghton Mifflin, 1981), 229.

32. *Transcript*, 7.

33. Stern, 250.

34. Burke, *Grammar of Motives*, 24.

35. *Transcript*, 8.

36. Ibid.

37. Ibid.

38. Ibid.

39. Ibid.

40. Ibid.

41. Ibid., 9.

42. Ibid.

43. Ibid., 10.

44. Ibid., 972.

45. Ibid., 8.

46. Ibid., 9.

47. Ibid.

48. Ibid.

49. Ibid., 10.

50. Ibid.

51. Ibid., 11.

52. Ibid., 13.

53. Ibid.

54. Ibid.

55. Ibid., 14.

56. Ibid.

57. Ibid.

58. Ibid., 14-17.

59. Ibid., 17.

60. Ibid., 15.

61. Ibid., 17.

62. Ibid., 19.

63. Ibid., 20.

64. Ibid.

65. Ibid.

Chapter 5

Oppenheimer's Public Life Rewritten: Analysis of the Decision Statements

On 12 April 1954, Oppenheimer faced the Personnel Security Board for the first time. Over the next nineteen days, board members Gordon Gray, Thomas Morgan, and Ward V. Evans, who had prestige and status equal to Oppenheimer's, heard testimony that, when compiled, filled a transcript of over 900 pages. The first entries were Nichols's letter of accusation and Oppenheimer's autobiographical reply. The Gray Board delivered its decision on 27 May 1954; the result emerged from its consideration of Nichols's charges, Oppenheimer's response, the supportive testimony, and other government records. The board voted two to one to deny reinstatement of Oppenheimer's security clearance.

Oppenheimer then requested that the AEC consider the case directly. On 29 June 1954, after reviewing the materials of the hearing, the AEC arrived at the same conclusion: Oppenheimer's continued employment presented a national security risk. Of the AEC commissioners, Lewis Strauss, Eugene M. Zuckert, and Joseph Campbell wrote the majority decision; Thomas Murray concurred but gave different reasons; and Henry DeWolf Smyth dissented.

The decisions to revoke Oppenheimer's security clearance are of special interest rhetorically because, although each group considered identical evidence and arrived at the same conclusion, the three decision statements used three different terminologies to label Oppenheimer as a security risk. Although interesting, the presence of a different terminology in each decision document is not surprising; defining a security risk, especially with regard to atomic secrets, was relatively new in 1954 and required terminological negotiation. Burke notes, "in an age of marked instability, of great and shifting contrasts, typical patterns of stimuli would be less likely to run through the group as a whole, or even a large part of it. Many of its stimulus-combinations will thus be unnamed.''[1] The stimulus combinations presented in the Oppenheimer case were essentially new. No precedents for a determination of their complexity existed. Both Oppenheimer and "security" were on trial. Terminological analysis of each decision statement reveals the divergent equations that defined security and thus labeled Oppenheimer a security risk. In the remainder of this chapter, I use terminological algebra to highlight the key definitions and turning points in each decision. First, the Gray-Morgan equation, "loyal, but a security risk," is examined. Then the AEC majority equation, "guilty in all relevant terms," is considered. And finally, terminological analysis reveals the central tenets of Murray's concurring equation, "disloyal, therefore a security risk."

THE GRAY-MORGAN EQUATION: LOYAL, BUT A SECURITY RISK

Gray and Morgan, the Personnel Security Board majority, introduced their findings and recommendations with a discussion of the "state of affairs" in the country.[2] As they bemoaned the "present peril" created by "repressive totalitarianism," they also hoped for a more positive future. In their hopefulness, they revealed their perspective on loyalty and security:

We share the hope that some day we may return to happier times when our free institutions are not threatened and a peaceful and just world order is not such a compelling principal preoccupation. . . . Then security will cease to be a central issue; . . . loyalty and security as concepts will cease to have restrictive implications.[3]

Two paragraphs later, Gray and Morgan noted that they were "acutely aware that in a very real sense this case put the security system of the United States on trial."[4] The context of the charges, a central factor in Oppenheimer's defense, clearly was a consideration for Gray and Morgan. However, their opening statement seemed somewhat foreboding for Oppenheimer because they indicated heightened requirements for loyalty and security.

Beyond the general orientation created in this section, the opening statement reveals at least two important characteristics of the Gray-Morgan terminology. Security, indeed, is questioned. It is not considered a known quantity. Although specific criteria are presented, security is, to some degree, negotiable. Initially, Gray and Morgan addressed the equation:

$$(?security) ? (?Oppenheimer)$$

In order to make a decision, they had to define both terms as well as the relationship between them.

Gray and Morgan also signaled a special connection between "security" and "loyalty" in their terminology. The terms are used in conjunction, not only in the passage already quoted, but in a subsequent passage as well: "We believe that loyalty and security can be examined within frameworks of the traditional and inviolable principles of American justice."[5] In the Gray-Morgan terminology, loyalty was as much at issue as security. Although "character" and "associations" also were noted as guiding terms, "loyalty" took on special significance in the document's introduction and appeared as a critical term in each section thereafter.

National Loyalty

"Loyalty" emerged as the pivotal term in the Gray-Morgan definition of security. As they stated in their conclusion, Oppenheimer's loyalty was the most serious question faced by the Personnel Security Board; it was perhaps even greater than security itself:

The most serious finding which this Board could make as a result of these proceedings would be that of disloyalty on the part of Dr. Oppenheimer to his country. For that reason, we have given particular attention to the question of his loyalty, and we have come to a clear conclusion, which should be reassuring to the people of this country, that he is a loyal citizen.[6]

Gray and Morgan arrived at the conclusion that Oppenheimer's loyalty had a positive value (+ Oppenheimer's loyalty) only after their in-depth analysis of loyalty and Oppenheimer's relation to it.

Before they discussed Oppenheimer's case in particular, Gray and Morgan first considered "the great issues and problems brought into focus by this case."[7] The first issue was posed as a question: "what, within the framework of this case, is meant by loyalty?"[8]

Gray and Morgan defined "disloyalty" (− disloyalty) first as an active betrayal of the U.S. government. "If a person is considered a security risk in terms of loyalty, the fact or possibility of active disloyalty is assumed, which would involve conduct giving some sort of aid and comfort to a foreign power."[9] Later in the document they called the positive form of this loyalty "love of country." The term seems to imply a purity of motivation: Individuals are loyal as long as they do not harm the United States *intentionally*. In the remainder of this analysis, this type of loyalty will be termed "national loyalty." Therefore:

$$(+ \text{national loyalty}) \neq (- \text{active aid to a foreign power})$$

Gray and Morgan valued Oppenheimer's loyalty positively in this sense. Given their argument that loyalty was crucial to security, Oppenheimer's positive loyalty would have led, seemingly, to a decision in his favor. However, Gray and Morgan argued that there were negative terms that out-weighed Oppenheimer's recognized loyalty, namely his character and associations. Regardless of his loyalty, therefore, Gray and Morgan did not recommend him for security clearance.

On the one hand, we find no evidence of disloyalty. Indeed, we have before us much responsible and positive evidence of the loyalty and love of country of the individual concerned. On the other hand, we do not believe that it has been demonstrated that Dr. Oppenheimer has been blameless in the matter of conduct, character, and associations.[10]

From this early position statement, Gray and Morgan's overall security equation was:

$(+\text{security}) \neq (-\text{character}) + (-\text{associations}) + (+\text{NATIONAL LOYALTY})$

This, however, is a simplistic account of the Gray-Morgan terminology. In order to understand their decision, the term "loyalty" and its relationships to other compository terms must be explored further.

Associations

Gray and Morgan accepted Oppenheimer's contextualization of his associations as past and naïve. Oppenheimer's associations might have fallen within Gray and Morgan's "national loyalty" definition, yet they accepted Oppenheimer's contention that people and terms change with scenes and that he had progressed beyond his misguided political adventures of the 1930s.

Stated in the context of this proceeding, must we accept the principle that once a Communist, always a Communist, once a fellow-traveler, always a fellow traveler? . . . The necessary but harsh requirements of security should not deny a man the right to have made a mistake, if its recurrence is so remote a possibility as to permit a comfortable prediction as to the sanity and correctness of future conduct.[11]

Later they stated, "We recognize that 1943 conduct cannot be judged solely in the light of 1954 conditions."[12] Although they found Nichols's accusations concerning Oppenheimer's 1930s communist associations to be true, Gray and Morgan, like Oppenheimer, granted them little significance. Gray and Morgan considered Oppenheimer "rehabilitated." They therefore found no negative implications for his associations and loyalty based on this evidence.

The Board believes . . . that there is no indication of disloyalty on the part of Dr. Oppenheimer by reason of any present Communist affiliation. . . . Furthermore, the Board had before it eloquent and convincing testimony of Dr. Oppenheimer's deep devotion to his country in recent years.[13]

Gray and Morgan argued that Oppenheimer's 1930s associations did not affect this "national loyalty" negatively. If anything, his associations were a matter in the past and were harmless in 1954. Despite their opening statement, which valued his associations negatively, to Gray and Morgan Oppenheimer's 1930s associations had been blameless and relatively unimportant. Oppenheimer's security sum, at this stage in the explanation, was:

$$(+ \text{SECURITY}) = (?\text{character}) + (1930s \text{ associations}) + (+ \text{NATIONAL LOYALTY})$$

This apparent contradiction surrounding his associations was only the first of several inconsistencies in the Gray-Morgan decision.

Unfortunately for Oppenheimer, Gray and Morgan did not stop with the question of associations. They also asked, "Can an individual be loyal to the United States and, nevertheless, be considered a security risk?"[14] They asked if other negative compository terms could outweigh positive national loyalty. In algebraic terms, they can be said to have pondered the possibility, for instance, that:

$$(+ \text{SECURITY}) \neq (- \text{character}) + (- \text{associations}) + (+ \text{NATIONAL LOYALTY})$$

Gray and Morgan answered their own question affirmatively. Conveniently, Oppenheimer's case demonstrated their hypothetical musings in actual terms. Although Oppenheimer's past communist associations were discounted, either his present associations or his character, if negative and significant, might outweigh his national loyalty and thereby negate his security sum. Recall that the preview to Gray and Morgan's decision suggested that Oppenheimer's character and associations were indeed negative and that their combined values outweighed his positive loyalty. All that remained was to explain the terms that spelled Oppenheimer's defeat.

Character and Persuasibility

Gray and Morgan argued that a person could violate security unintentionally from personal weakness. In the Gray-Morgan terminology and in security statutes, a "character flaw" such as inordinate use of alcohol or drugs, personal indiscretion, homosexuality, or emotional instability made a person a security risk. Therefore, regardless of a person's national loyalty, if a personal weakness was present, that person was deemed a security risk. Positive character was a necessary but not sufficient condition for a positive security sum. In algebraic terms, the resulting equation would be:

(+SECURITY) ≠ (−character) + (+associations) + (+NATIONAL LOYALTY)

If that equation is further defined, the following relationships result:

(+security) ≠ (−character)

(+character) ≠ (−personal weakness)

(+security) = (+character) ≠(−drug abuse)

(+security) = (+character) ≠ (−emotional instability)

(+security) = (+character) ≠ (−personal indiscretion)

(+security) = (+character) ≠ *and so on*

Therefore, any one of the personal weaknesses outlined in the statute could result in a negative security evaluation.

In their comparison of these standards to Oppenheimer's actions, Gray and Morgan noted that "Dr. Oppenheimer seems to have had a high degree of discretion reflecting an unusual ability to keep to himself vital secrets."[15] He had never demonstrated a flawed character or a flawed loyalty. He had never intentionally or unintentionally harmed security. Oppenheimer appeared to pass the test on both character and national loyalty; yet in the very next sentence, Gray and Morgan asserted that Oppenheimer had displayed a "weakness," as described in Executive Order 10450: "However, we do find suggestions of a tendency to be coerced, or at least influenced in conduct over a period of years."[16] They then noted instances in which other persons had persuaded Oppenheimer to change a previously stated position. For instance, Gray and Morgan suggested that Edward U. Condon, a well-known scientist, had had undue influence over Oppenheimer:

By his own testimony, Dr. Oppenheimer was led to protest the induction into military service of Giovanni Rossi Lomanitz in 1943 by the outraged intercession of Dr. Condon. It is to be remembered that, at this time, Dr. Oppenheimer knew of Lomanitz's connections and of his indiscretions.[17]

Gray and Morgan argued that Oppenheimer's character was flawed because he was too persuasible.

(−Oppenheimer's character) = (−susceptibility to influence)

Yet Gray and Morgan apparently felt that their negative evaluation of character was insufficient to negate Oppenheimer's security sum. After they made the allegation, they backed down. They used the same evidence, however, to challenge Oppenheimer's loyalty to the security system.

Loyalty to the Security System

Gray and Morgan used evidence of Oppenheimer's inconsistencies to expand the requirements of security and loyalty. While somewhat reluctant to impugn Oppenheimer's character, the Personnel Security Board majority made definite arguments to negate Oppenheimer's loyalty to the security system.

Whether the incidents referred to clearly indicate a susceptibility to influence or coercion within the meaning of the criteria or whether they simply reflect very bad judgment, they clearly raise the question of Dr. Oppenheimer's understanding, acceptance, and enthusiastic support of the security system.[18]

The Gray-Morgan terminology represented yet another term also found in Oppenheimer's terminology—"loyalty to the security system." Recall that in Oppenheimer's defense

$$(loyalty) = (loyalty\ to\ country) + (loyalty\ to\ security\ system)$$
$$+ (administrative\ loyalty)$$

Part of loyalty to the security system, in the Gray-Morgan terminology, was, as Oppenheimer had argued, a subordination of personal judgment. They held that

security must involve a subordination of personal judgment as to the security status of an individual against a professional judgment. . . . It must entail a wholehearted commitment to the preservation of the security system and the avoidance of conduct tending to confuse or obstruct.[19]

Recall that Oppenheimer asserted that he had, in fact, subordinated his personal judgment to the security system on several occasions. He argued that:

$$security\ system > personal\ judgment$$

and

$$(+Oppenheimer's\ loyalty) = (+NATIONAL\ LOYALTY)$$
$$+ (loyalty\ to\ security\ system)$$

Gray and Morgan adopted the structure, but not the direction, of Oppenheimer's equational system. They challenged the value that he assigned to his loyalty to the security system. They believed that Oppenheimer had not subordinated his personal judgment to the security system. They held that

beginning with the Chevalier incident he has repeatedly exercised an arrogance of judgment with respect to loyalty and reliability of other citizens to an extent which has frustrated and at times impeded the workings of the system.[20]

In Gray and Morgan's estimation, Oppenheimer's behavior was captured in the equation

$$\text{personal judgment} > \text{security system}$$

Oppenheimer had placed himself above regulations. Gray and Morgan especially noted the Chevalier Incident, because, while under oath, Oppenheimer had admitted that he had lied to protect Chevalier.

Oppenheimer's lies furthered the negative estimation of his character. Gray and Morgan, though concerned about the lies, seemed more worried about Oppenheimer's tendency to favor friends over security requirements. As Gray expressed in the hearing, "it would appear that at that time and under those circumstances within the framework of loyalty generally— loyalty to an individual, broader loyalty to a country. . . . In that case considerations of personal loyalty might have outweighed the broader loyalties."[21] Gray created a hierarchy of loyalties to which Oppenheimer apparently had not conformed. The equation that represents that hierarchy is:

$$+ \text{ national loyalty} = \text{loyalty to security system} > \text{loyalty to friends}$$

Oppenheimer gave credence to Gray's interpretation in an explanation of his behavior:

It was a matter of conflict for me and I found myself, I believe, trying to give a tip to the intelligence people without realizing that when you give a tip you must tell the whole story. When I was asked to elaborate, I started off on a false pattern. I may add 1 or 2 things. Chevalier was a friend of mine."[22]

From Oppenheimer's own admission that a hierarchy of loyalties had affected his actions, Gray and Morgan found his conduct "not clearly consistent with the interests of security."[23] Moreover, Oppenheimer's loyalty to Chevalier had continued throughout the intervening years. Gray and Morgan found his continued association with Chevalier as yet another violation of security requirements.

It is not important to determine that Dr. Oppenheimer discussed with Chevalier matters of concern to the security of the United States. What is important is that Chevalier's Communist background and activities were known to Dr. Oppenheimer. While he says he believes that Chevalier is not now a Communist, his association with him, on what could not be considered a casual basis, is not the kind of thing that our security system permits.[24]

Based on this statement, Oppenheimer's associations were negative because they violated security standards. His character was negative because he was susceptible to influence and had lied repeatedly to officials. His loyalty to the security system was negative because he had made a decision in which he favored his personal judgment over security requirements. In Gray and Morgan's estimation, his overall security equation was:

$$(+ \text{security}) \neq (- \text{character}) + (- 1954 \text{ associations})$$
$$+ (+ \text{NATIONAL LOYALTY}) + (- \text{loyalty to security})$$

Opposition to the H-bomb

Gray and Morgan did not incorporate the H-bomb evidence into their terminology. Its absence may indicate the volatility of the accusation. The Personnel Security Board majority adopted Oppenheimer's equation structure and much of his argument but did not agree with the evaluations he attributed within that structure to describe his actions in the 1949 H-bomb controversy.

Gray and Morgan felt that Oppenheimer's opposition to the hydrogen bomb "involved no lack of loyalty to the United States."[25] Gray and Morgan referred to testimony from H-bomb advocates consonant with their view. For instance, Edward Teller, the "father of the hydrogen bomb," believed that Oppenheimer was loyal.

I believe, and that is merely a question of belief and there is no expertness, no real information behind it, that Dr. Oppenheimer's character is such that he would not knowingly or willingly do anything that is designed to endanger the safety of this country.[26]

For Gray and Morgan, however, Oppenheimer's relationship to hydrogen bomb development did not end "simply with the finding that his conduct was not motivated by disloyalty," but that, whatever his motivation, security interests were affected. Here Gray and Morgan accepted the terms present in testimony by Kenneth Pitzer, "I have great difficulty believing that the program would have had certain difficulties that it did have at the time if he [Oppenheimer] had enthusiastically urged individuals to participate in the program."[27] Gray and Morgan wrote, "We believe that, had Dr. Oppenheimer given his enthusiastic support to the program, a concerted effort would have been initiated at an earlier date."[28] In their estimation:

$$(+ \text{organization loyalty}) = (+ \text{enthusiastic support of administration goals})$$

$$(+ \text{security}) \neq (- \text{organizational loyalty})$$

$$(+ \text{security}) \neq (- \text{lack of enthusiasm for administrative goals})$$

$$(- \text{lack of enthusiasm for administrative goals}) = (- \text{organizational loyalty})$$

$$(+ \text{security}) \neq (- \text{Oppenheimer's organizational loyalty})$$

The board members made it clear that they believed that Oppenheimer's right to an opinion was not in question, but rather that "he may have departed his role as scientific advisor to exercise highly persuasive influence in matters in which his convictions were not necessarily a reflection of technical judgment."[29] In other words, scientific advisors may hold any opinions they wish, but must openly and enthusiastically support administration goals, regardless of personal feelings to the contrary. Recall that government standards and Oppenheimer's terminology both asserted that

$$\text{scientific advisor} \neq \text{military advisor}$$
$$\text{scientific advisor} \neq \text{political advisor}$$

Gray and Morgan went beyond even those divisions. In their view, Oppenheimer's crime was an organizational one—he had not adopted the terms of the administration. He was, so to speak, guilty of "bucking the system," regardless of his arguments to the contrary. In the Gray-Morgan terminology, such activities could not fit into a positive security sum. Oppenheimer may have had loyal intentions, but his *actions* were disloyal in yet another sense. His loyalty equation was:

$$(-\text{Oppenheimer's loyalty}) = (+\text{NATIONAL LOYALTY})$$
$$+ (-\text{loyalty to security system}) + (-\text{organizational loyalty})$$

"Loyalty," the term that appeared to be the most supportive of Oppenheimer in the opening of the Gray-Morgan opinion, turned out to be perhaps the most damaging evaluation.

Given their negative recommendation and their derogatory descriptions of Oppenheimer's actions, one comment in particular is noteworthy for its apparent inconsistency. Gray and Morgan openly stated that an "alternative recommendation," apparently a positive overall equation, could have described the case. "It seemed to us that an alternative recommendation would be possible, if we were allowed to exercise mature practical judgment without the rigid circumscription of regulations and criteria established for us."[30] Gray and Morgan apparently believed that Oppenheimer deserved clearance, but felt compelled by documented standards to make the opposite recommendation. Their statement is noteworthy not only because of the equivocality it introduced into the Gray-Morgan opinion, but also because it demonstrates that the judges' interpretation of their role and their understanding of the requirements made of them by the AEC figured significantly in the decision they made.

Nichols, Oppenheimer, and Gray and Morgan selected "character," "associations," and "loyalty" as the compository terms of "security." The regulations and criteria were cited in each document as well. However, the reading of the documents by Gray and Morgan made the terms "loyalty" and "security" more restrictive than they were in either of their personal terminologies. They applied the terminologies of the Personnel Security Board members rather than the terminologies of private citizens, believing that their personal judgment should be subordinated to their duty to the security system. They adapted their terminologies to the positions they held. They applied the same standard to their official function that they applied to Oppenheimer's advisory role. The restrictions were a terminological choice made in the context of the personnel security hearing.

Nevertheless, the criteria need not have restricted their decision. Ironically, they could have selected passages from the AEC security criteria that would have allowed Oppenheimer's clearance. For example, that document held, "The facts of each case must be carefully weighed and determination made in the light of all the information presented, whether favorable or unfavorable. . . . The decision as to security clearance is an overall commonsense judgment."[31] The "mature practical judgment," the decision Gray and Morgan apparently wanted to make, *was* allowed by the AEC security criteria. This directive, however, was used only in the dissenting opinion by Smyth, who argued,

Application of this standard of overall commonsense judgment to the whole record destroys any pattern of suspicious conduct or catalog of falsehoods and evasions, and leaves a picture of Dr. Oppenheimer as an able, imaginative human being with normal human weaknesses and failings.[32]

Had Gray and Morgan adopted this admonishment, their security equation for Oppenheimer might have been positive. Unfortunately for Oppenheimer, however, Gray and Morgan constructed a different, and more damaging, set of terminological relationships.

While Gray and Morgan fought to support Oppenheimer but labeled him both loyal and a security risk, the AEC majority, Oppenheimer's second set of judges, apparently felt no desire to protect the prestigious and respected "father of the atomic bomb." The AEC majority applied the documented criteria stringently and found Oppenheimer "guilty in all relevant terms."

THE AEC MAJORITY EQUATION: GUILTY IN ALL RELEVANT TERMS

At the outset of their statement, it becomes clear that AEC commissioners Strauss, Zuckert, and Campbell adopted "character," "associations," and "loyalty" as the terms crucial to security. They weighted the terms, however, in a much different way from the Oppenheimer case rhetors who had preceded them.

The Atomic Energy Act of 1946 lays upon the Commission the duty to reach a determination as to "the character, associations, and loyalty" of individuals engaged in
the work of the Commission. Thus, disloyalty would be one basis for disqualification, but it is only one. Substantial defects of character and imprudent and dangerous associations . . . are also reasons for disqualification.[33]

Note the change in the equation from Nichols's accusations, from Oppenheimer's reply, and even from the Gray-Morgan report. For the majority,
loyalty, a primary and significant concern in the other positions, was no
more important than character and associations. In fact, the AEC majority
arrived at a negative judgment without use of the term "loyalty," which did
not appear again after the opening passage, quoted above. Moreover, the
majority asserted that if any one of the compository terms was negative, the
security sum also must be negative. Their terminology proposed that

$$(+\text{security}) = (?\text{character}) + (?\text{associations}) + (?\text{loyalty})$$

$$(+\text{security}) \neq (-\text{character}) + (+\text{associations}) + (+\text{loyalty})$$

$$(+\text{security}) \neq (+\text{character}) + (-\text{associations}) + (+\text{loyalty})$$

$$(+\text{security}) \neq (+\text{character}) + (+\text{associations}) + (-\text{loyalty})$$

The AEC majority felt that only two equations were relevant to the Oppenheimer case:

$$(+\text{security}) ? (?\text{character})$$

$$(+\text{security}) ? (?\text{associations})$$

In the majority terminology, if either character or associations were negative, Oppenheimer was a security risk.

Not only did the AEC majority discount the relevance of loyalty, but also
they dropped the H-bomb issue. They, like Gray and Morgan, supported
Oppenheimer's right to his opinion. Moreover, they did not consider his
degree of contribution to H-bomb development, let alone the "enthusiasm"
of his actions, relevant to the case.

Neither in the deliberation by the full Commission nor in the review of the Gray
board was importance attached to the opinions of Dr. Oppenheimer as they bore
upon the 1949 debate within the Government on the question of whether the United
States should proceed with the thermonuclear program. In this debate, Dr. Oppenheimer was, of course, entitled to his opinion.[34]

That was the only reference to Oppenheimer's opinions concerning the
hydrogen bomb in the AEC majority report.

Once loyalty and organizational loyalty had been removed from the discussion, the majority explained the decision under two parallel headings:

(1) "as to 'character' " and (2) "as to 'associations.' "

Character

The AEC majority asserted that "Dr. Oppenheimer is not entitled to the continued confidence of the Government and of this Commission because of the proof of fundamental defects in his 'character'."[35] To support this strong allegation against Oppenheimer, the majority cited six instances in which Oppenheimer had falsified or misrepresented matters that involved security obligations. The first was the Chevalier Incident.

It is not clear today whether the account Dr. Oppenheimer gave to Colonel Pash in 1943 concerning the Chevalier incident or the story he told the Gray Board last month is the true version. If Dr. Oppenheimer lied in 1943, as he now says he did, he committed the crime of knowingly making false and material statements to a Federal officer. If he lied to the Board, he committed perjury in 1954.[36]

Four other instances involved Oppenheimer's equivocations about persons known to him as Communists. The final case suggested that Oppenheimer had made false statements concerning the unanimity of the general advisory committee's 1949 H-bomb recommendation. The AEC majority was not concerned about the recommendation's content, but about the fact that Oppenheimer had misrepresented the proceedings. The Commissioners then stated that "the catalog does not end with these six examples. The work of Military Intelligence, the Federal Bureau of Investigation, and the Atomic Energy Commission—all, at one time or another have felt the effect of his falsehoods, evasions, and misrepresentations."[37]

The AEC majority, in effect, instituted a well-known terminological process—they called Oppenheimer a liar. Since

$$(+ \text{character}) \neq (- \text{dishonesty})$$

in the terminologies of American society and the AEC itself, these assertions negated Oppenheimer's character:

$$(- \text{Oppenheimer's character}) = (- \text{dishonesty})$$

One of the AEC's preliminary equations, then, was rounded out:

$$(+ \text{security}) = (- \text{character})$$

For the AEC majority, these allegations alone warranted Oppenheimer's removal from government service. His associations, however, reinforced the negative security sum created by character and, as such, only furthered the AEC argument.

Associations

The AEC majority, in an explanation similar to that used by Gray and Morgan, also impugned Oppenheimer's associations.

In respect to the criterion of "associations," we find that his associations with persons known to him to be Communists have extended far beyond the tolerable limits of prudence and self-restraint which are to be expected of one holding the high positions that the Government has continuously entrusted to him since 1942.[38]

Like Oppenheimer himself, the AEC majority did not consider past associations alone to be a matter of concern. They, too, considered the 1930s as the context for most of Oppenheimer's communist affiliations. It was not past associations that were problematic; in 1954 Oppenheimer had still not broken off all associations with Communists. As Gray and Morgan had pointed out, Oppenheimer had maintained his friendship with Chevalier:

Dr. Oppenheimer's early Communist associations are not in themselves a controlling reason for our decision. They take on importance in the context of his persistent and continuing association with Communists, including his admitted meetings with Haakon Chevalier in Paris as recently as last December—the same individual who had been intermediary for the Soviet Consulate in 1943.[39]

In the majority opinion:

$$(-\text{Oppenheimer's associations}) = (-\text{communist associations})$$

$$(+\text{security}) \neq (-\text{character}) + (-\text{associations})$$

The term "loyalty," critical in all other explanations of Oppenheimer's security sum, had no bearing on the determination by the AEC majority. A term that essentially determined the sum in one evaluation became a null factor in another. Both equations reached a negative sum; however, a decision is not characterized merely by its outcome, but by the terminological path that leads to that outcome as well.

The Oppenheimer case was interpreted by one more terminological path that led to a negative result—Murray's concurring equation. His overall security equation was much simpler than in the preceding explanations. Murray believed that

$$\text{security} = \text{loyalty}$$

MURRAY'S CONCURRING EQUATION: DISLOYAL, THEREFORE, A SECURITY RISK

Murray argued that only one term was relevant to the Oppenheimer case: "loyalty." For Murray, "loyalty" and "security" were equivalent terms.

The primary issue is the meaning of loyalty. I shall define this concept concretely within the conditions created by the present crisis of national and international security. When loyalty is thus concretely defined and when all the evidence is carefully considered in the light of this definition, it will be evident that Dr. Oppenheimer was disloyal.[40]

Murray began his exposition of "loyalty" in broad terms. "The idea of loyalty has emotional connotations; it is related to the idea of love, a man's love of his country."[41] He then narrowed the definition to its derivation. "The English word 'loyal' comes to us from the Latin adjective 'legalis,' which means 'according to the law.'" To be loyal, in Webster's definition, is to be "faithful to the lawful government or to the sovereign to whom one is subject."[42] To this point, Murray's equations had unfolded as:

$$(+\text{security}) = (+\text{loyalty})$$

$$(+\text{security}) = (+\text{faithfulness to law})$$

Murray expands on the legal definition to include "the fact of the Communist conspiracy."

Government, because it is lawful, has the right and the responsibility to protect itself against the action of those who would subvert it. The cooperative effort of the citizen with the rightful action of American Government in its discharge of this primary responsibility also belongs to the very substance of American loyalty. This is the crucial principle in the present case. . . . The premise of the concrete, contemporary definition of loyalty is the fact of the Communist conspiracy.[43]

Security, therefore, involved a citizen's active fight against communism.

$$(+\text{security}) = (+\text{citizen's cooperation with government})$$

$$(+\text{security}) = (+\text{citizen's cooperation with government to thwart} \\ \text{communist infiltration})$$

Through substitution, Murray developed a narrow standard of loyalty for all Americans.

Murray made further specifications for government employees. With regard to security, Murray said that "their faithfulness to the lawful government of the United States, that is to say their loyalty, must be judged by the hard standard of their obedience to security regulations."[44] His modified equation was:

$$(+\text{security}) = (+\text{faithfulness to security procedures})$$

While the term "loyalty to security system" had appeared in the terminology of Oppenheimer and also that of Gray and Morgan, it had not held the significance that it held for Murray. "Loyalty to the security system" was the only consideration in Murray's security equation. Given Murray's security equation, Oppenheimer's fate was set. He had violated security procedure more than once. It was a matter of record.

The existence of the security regulations which surround the atomic energy program puts to those who participate in the program a stern test of loyalty. Dr. Oppenheimer failed that test. The record of his actions reveals a frequent and deliberate disregard of those security regulations which restrict a man's associations.[45]

Murray concluded that

(Oppenheimer's record) = ($-$ faithfulness to security procedures)

($+$ security) $\neq$ ($-$ faithfulness to security procedures).

Murray then returned to his original contention that security = loyalty. Through substitution, he declared that Oppenheimer was disloyal. "These regulations are the special test of the loyalty of the American citizen who serves his government in the sensitive area of the Atomic Energy Program. Dr. Oppenheimer did not meet this decisive test. He was disloyal."[46] What Gray and Morgan had worked so hard to avoid, Murray stated flatly in his concurring opinion.

($+$ security) = ($+$ loyalty)

($+$ security) = ($+$ loyalty) = ($+$ faithfulness to security procedures)

***

($-$ Oppenheimer's record) = ($-$ faithfulness to security procedures)

($-$ Oppenheimer's record) = ($-$ disloyalty)

***

($+$ security) $\neq$ ($-$ loyalty)

($+$ security) $\neq$ ($-$ Oppenheimer)

THE JUDGES' RESPONSES TO THE ISSUES

A comparison of the decision statements suggests that while Nichols's accusations and Oppenheimer's defense affected the case's outcome, the judges constructed highly individual terminologies as well. The key terms "character," "associations," and "loyalty" appeared consistently in the decisions, but their meanings and their significance varied from rhetor to

Figure 5.1
The Gray-Morgan Equation

Decision Overview

```
    (+national loyalty)  ≠  (-active aid to a foriegn power)
(+security)  ≠  (-character)  +  (-associations)  +  (+NATIONAL LOYALTY)
```

Loyalty and Associations

```
        (+1930s associations)  and  (+NATIONAL LOYALTY)
(+SECURITY)  ≠  (-character)  +  (+1930s associations)  +
                    (+NATIONAL LOYALTY)
```

Loyalty and Character

```
(+SECURITY)  ≠  (-character)  +  (+associations)  +  (+NATIONAL LOYALTY)
                (+SECURITY)  ≠  (-character)
                (+character)  ≠  (-any personal weakness)
                (+SECURITY)  ≠  (-any personal weakness)
    (-Oppenheimer's character)  =  (-susceptability to influence)
```

Loyalty and the Security System

```
loyalty  =  (NATIONAL LOYALTY)  +  (loyalty to the security system)
  loyalty to the security system  =  (security system > personal
                                        judgment)
NATIONAL LOYALTY  =  (loyalty to the security system > loyalty to
                                    friends)
  (Oppenheimer's loyalty)  =  (+NATIONAL LOYALTY)  +  (-loyalty to
                                    security)
    (+SECURITY)  ≠  (-character)  +  (-1954 associations)  +
    (NATIONAL LOYALTY)  +  (-loyalty to the security system)
```

National Loyalty and Organizational Loyalty

```
    (+organizational loyalty)  =  (enthusiastic support of
                            administration goals)
            (+SECURITY)  ≠  (-organizational loyalty)
(+SECURITY)  ≠  (non-enthusiastic support of administration goals)
(Oppenheimer's loyalty)  =  (+NATIONAL LOYALTY)  +  (-loyalty to
    security system)  +  (-organizational loyalty)
```

The Gray-Morgan Decision

```
    (+SECURITY)  ≠  (-character)  +  (-associations)  +
    (+NATIONAL LOYALTY)  +  (-loyalty to security system)  +
            (-organizational loyalty)
```

rhetor. Figures 5.1, 5.2, and 5.3 summarize the decision statements.

Like Nichols and Oppenheimer, both the Personnel Security Board majority and the AEC majority recognized "character," "associations," and "loyalty" as the compository terms of "security." Nevertheless, the meanings attributed and the values assigned to the terms differed greatly. Gray and Morgan emphasized loyalty in many forms. They adopted Oppen-

Figure 5.2
The AEC Majority Equation

<u>Preliminary Equations</u>

(+security) $\boxed{?}$ (?character) + (?associations) + (?loyalty)

(+security) $\boxed{?}$ (?character)

(+security) $\boxed{?}$ (?associations)

<u>As to "Character"</u>

(+character) = (+honesty)
(-Oppenheimer's character) = (-dishonesty)
(+security) ≠ (-character)

<u>As to "Associations"</u>

(Oppenheimer's associations) = (communist associations)
(-Oppenheimer's associations) = (-communist associations)

<u>Decision</u>

(+security) ≠ (-character) + (-associations)

Figure 5.3
Murray's Concurring Equation

<u>Loyalty for All Americans</u>

(+security) = (+loyalty)
(+security) = (+person's love of country)
(+security) = (+faithfulness to government)
(+security) = (+citizen's cooperation with government)
(+security) = (+citizen's cooperation with government to thwart
Communist infiltration)

<u>Loyalty for Civil Servants</u>

(+security) = (faithfulness to the security system)

<u>Loyalty for Oppenheimer</u>

(Oppenheimer's record) = (faithfulness to the security system)
(-Oppenheimer's record) = (-loyalty)

<u>Decision</u>

(+security) ≠ (-loyalty)

heimer's equational structures and accepted much of his argument as well. They discounted his early communist associations. They, too, believed that a person could be rehabilitated. However, they reversed his explanations in terms of "loyalty to the security system" and "organizational loyalty." They also refused to overlook his contradictions and his continued associations with Chevalier.

The AEC majority negated Oppenheimer's character and associations for much the same reasons, citing Oppenheimer's "willful and arrogant disregard for security." Unlike the Personnel Security Board majority, however, the commissioners gave no significance to the discussion of the hydrogen bomb. Indeed, in each of the AEC reports, Nichols's allegations about Oppenheimer's involvement in the H-bomb dispute were disregarded. Perhaps the most surprising was the AEC majority's lack of attention to loyalty; the term that was most complex and decisive in the Gray-Morgan terminology was omitted by the AEC majority.

Murray agreed that the hydrogen bomb issue had had little to do with the determination to be made, and he thereby moved closer to the terminology of his fellow commissioners, agreeing with Gray and Morgan that "loyalty" was the pivotal term. His definition of loyalty, however, quickly diverged from the Gray-Morgan terminology. What Oppenheimer, Gray, and Morgan had called "loyalty to the security system" was simply "loyalty" for Murray. For him there were no other standards; loyalty *was* security. So, while Gray and Morgan called Oppenheimer loyal and the AEC majority ignored Oppenheimer's loyalty, Murray made the definitive claim that Oppenheimer was disloyal.

Many possible explanations underlie the diversity of the decision terminologies and their negative implications for Oppenheimer's life. A discussion of those possibilities follows in Chapter 6.

NOTES

1. Kenneth Burke, *Permanence and Change: An Anatomy of Purpose*, 3d ed. (Berkeley: University of California Press, 1984), 32-33.

2. U.S. Atomic Energy Commission, *In the Matter of J. Robert Oppenheimer: Texts of Principal Documents and Letters of Personnel Security Board, May 27, 1954, through June 29; 1954* (Washington, D.C.: Government Printing Office, 1954), 1. Hereafter noted as *Documents*.

3. Ibid., 1.

4. Ibid.

5. Ibid., 2.

6. Ibid., 21.

7. Ibid., 14.

8. Ibid.

9. Ibid.

10. Ibid., 13.

11. Ibid., 14.

12. Ibid., 15.

13. Ibid., 19.

14. Ibid., 15.

15. Ibid., 20.

16. Ibid.

17. Ibid.

18. Ibid.

19. Ibid., 15.

20. Ibid., 20.

21. U.S. Atomic Energy Commission, *In the Matter of J. Robert Oppenheimer: Transcript of Hearing before Personnel Security Board* (Washington, D.C.: Government Printing Office, 1954), 251. Hereafter noted as *Transcript.*

22. Ibid., 888.

23. *Documents*, 21.

24. Ibid.

25. Ibid., 19.

26. *Transcript*, 726.

27. Ibid., 106.

28. *Documents*, 19.

29. Ibid.

30. Ibid., 13.

31. See U.S. Atomic Energy Commission, "Personnel Security Clearance Criteria for Determining Eligibility," *Federal Register* 15 (1950), 8094.

32. *Documents*, 67.

33. Ibid., 51.

34. Ibid.

35. Ibid.

36. Ibid., 53.

37. Ibid.

38. Ibid., 51.

39. Ibid., 54.

40. Ibid., 60.

41. Ibid., 61.

42. Ibid.

43. Ibid.

44. Ibid., 62.

45. Ibid., 63.

46. Ibid.

Chapter 6

Conclusions Drawn

Although the Oppenheimer case involved official and unofficial acts that spanned two turbulent decades, only in late 1954 did the public get its first glimpse at the historical record that revolved around one man, perhaps America's most prominent scientist, J. Robert Oppenheimer.

The record began with Nichols's presentation of "derogatory information" from Oppenheimer's past. He adopted the terms traditionally used by the FBI in security investigations; attacks on "character," "associations," and "loyalty" guided his charges. He quoted Executive Order 10450, the Atomic Energy Act of 1946, and the AEC Criteria for Determining Eligibility for Security Clearance—documents that listed the government's specific investigatory categories and the directives to be used in identifying security risks. He used these documented standards to round out his position strategically. Nichols emphasized the highly negative value attributed to "communism" at the height of the McCarthy "red scare." He then listed cases in which Oppenheimer had associated with known Communists, so that the negative evaluation was linked to Oppenheimer through his associations. Oppenheimer's character was impugned as well. The Chevalier Incident and the H-bomb controversy both demonstrated, in Nichols's estimation, an inconsistency between Oppenheimer's words and his actions. Nichols implied that Oppenheimer could not be trusted. In the end, Nichols challenged Oppenheimer's "veracity, conduct, and even his loyalty." These charges shook Oppenheimer's previously untouched pedestal. Individuals outside the AEC and scientific circles, and some in both arenas, had never

heard of the Chevalier Incident, of Oppenheimer's past and suspect affiliations, or of the hydrogen bomb controversy.

Oppenheimer's reply followed Nichols's accusations in the record created
by the Personnel Security Board. Apparently Oppenheimer still had much
to learn politically, as will be discussed below, because he responded within
the framework created by Nichols. He answered the charges, not in his own
terminology, but literally in Nichols's terms. Oppenheimer, like Nichols,
addressed "character," "associations," and "loyalty," but unlike Nichols,
he valued each set positively in relation to his own case. Each term was
addressed in context. Oppenheimer used an autobiographical, "whole
man" strategy.

Oppenheimer recast his 1930s communist associations as harmless. In his
view they were merely manifestations of his search for a political identity.
He also divided associations from "loyalty. While Nichols linked
Communists with disloyalty, Oppenheimer argued that Communists could
feel deeply committed to the U.S. government. He reiterated his "love of
country" at several points and extended his "loyalty" to the security system
and to the organizational hierarchy of which he was a part. Nichols had not
argued in these terms. Oppenheimer introduced loyalty to the security
system and organizational loyalty into the overall security equation.

To uphold his loyalty to the security system, Oppenheimer cited specific
instances in which he had subordinated his personal judgment to security
requirements. He apologized for the Chevalier Incident and assured his
judges that he had learned from his mistakes. Oppenheimer argued that his
organizational loyalty was impeccable. He rejected Nichols's characterization of his role in the hydrogen bomb's development, stating unequivocally
that he had not opposed hydrogen bomb development once it was a matter
of policy. To support his assertions, Oppenheimer defined the appropriate
scientific advisory role as technical—not political, military, or ethical—and
then described his particularly troublesome opinions as essentially technical
misgivings. He said he knew his "place" in the executive hierarchy. Oppenheimer ended his autobiographical letter with the proposition that he had
learned from his mistakes and that his experience made him a more
"secure" employee than he had been at any previous time.

The Personnel Security Board, Oppenheimer's first set of judges,
accepted much of his explanation. They clearly valued his contributions,
and they found his loyalty to the United States, the most critical issue in
their view, unquestionable. They commended Oppenheimer's discretion.
The Gray Board majority also agreed that Oppenheimer's 1930s communist
associations carried no negative implications for security. Yet even with these
"positive" evaluations, extenuating factors disturbed Gray and Morgan.

For instance, they said that Oppenheimer exhibited a susceptibility to
influence, although he had never actually revealed any classified information. His character, therefore, was negatively valued. Although he had

repented his Chevalier Incident mistakes, Oppenheimer had not broken off his friendship with Chevalier. While Gray and Morgan could overlook Oppenheimer's early associations as youthful indiscretions, they could not accept this current communist association. Oppenheimer's associations, therefore, also were negative. Gray and Morgan, like Oppenheimer, felt that loyalty to the security system and organizational loyalty were relevant to the security equation. Like Oppenheimer, they cited specific instances to support their position. The Gray-Morgan position, however, was the exact opposite of Oppenheimer's in its assigned values. They believed that Oppenheimer had not subordinated his personal judgment to security and that he had violated the organizational hierarchy. Gray and Morgan negated both Oppenheimer's loyalty to the security system and his organizational loyalty. Despite his many positive qualities, Gray and Morgan found Oppenheimer a security risk.

The AEC majority, Oppenheimer's second group of judges, adhered the most closely to documented standards. They, too, used "character," "associations," and "loyalty" as guiding terms. In the AEC majority terminology, however, if any one of security's compository terms was negative, the individual under investigation must be found a security risk. In the Oppenheimer case, therefore, the AEC majority considered only character and associations; loyalty was dropped from the security equation. The AEC majority also rejected Nichols's charges concerning Oppenheimer's involvement with the H-bomb decision. They considered Oppenheimer's personal opinions irrelevant to his security sum. The remaining terms and evidence led the AEC majority to a harsh recommendation. They found Oppenheimer's character defective, because he had lied to government officials on several occasions. Moreover, they said he had showed a "willful disregard for security." Like Gray and Morgan, the AEC majority felt that Oppenheimer's past associations, in and of themselves, carried no negative implications for security. However, given Oppenheimer's continued associations with Chevalier, they found his 1954 associations negative as well. In the estimation of the AEC majority, Oppenheimer was a security risk.

Murray agreed that Oppenheimer was a security risk. The reasons behind his decision, however, rested on "loyalty," the term his fellow commissioners had ignored. For Murray, loyalty was more than love of country. In its most specific sense, loyalty meant a "citizen's cooperation with government to thwart Communist infiltration." For a civil servant, loyalty demanded strict adherence to the security system. Since Oppenheimer had violated the security system more than once, he had failed to meet the loyalty standard. Murray believed that Oppenheimer was disloyal, and therefore a security risk.

The Oppenheimer case record exhibited twists and turns, many of which confounded, and some of which infuriated, observers at the time. As yet another examination of the Oppenheimer case record, this book had two initial purposes: (1) to explain why the accusations against Oppenheimer triumphed over his defense and (2) to refine a method that permits examination of terminological choice. At the outset of this work, I suggested that a comparison of the accusation, defense, and decision statements would reveal key points of similarity and dissimilarity and would be the basis for an explanation of the outcome. These key points and explanations now warrant discussion.

EVALUATION OF THE OPPENHEIMER CASE STRATEGIES

In an evaluation of the strategic rhetorical choices made in the Oppenheimer case, credit first must be given to Nichols, for choosing terms that targeted Oppenheimer's vulnerabilities and called upon the rhetorical forces of the times. By carefully indicating the standards relevant to the case, Nichols guided the direction of the hearing and the ultimate outcome. Oppenheimer's associations were especially useful to Nichols, since Oppenheimer could not deny factual information found in the FBI file. Neither could Oppenheimer deny his improprieties in the Chevalier Incident. They, too, were a matter of record. Oppenheimer's past offered obvious weaknesses.

Because of the political context in which they were presented, the "associations" charges, despite their simplicity, carried great rhetorical power. Nichols connected Oppenheimer with the most negative term available at the time: "communism." Nichols asserted that

$$Oppenheimer = (-communist)$$

"Communism," a specific form of un-American behavior, argues Richard M. Weaver, was the unrivaled devil term in 1953. " 'Un-American' is the ultimate in negation. . . . 'Communist' is beyond any rival the devil term and as such it is employed even by the American president when he feels the need of a strong rhetorical point."[1] The threat of communism needed no explicit definition or discussion. While Oppenheimer avoided the House Un-American Activities Committee and McCarthy, he could not dodge the implications of that terminology. He could not remove "communism" from his record, however distant and changed his associations might be. Nichols's strong introduction of the term into the hearing immediately placed Oppenheimer at a disadvantage.

Perhaps even more significant was Nichols's introduction of the H-bomb controversy into the charges. Stern suggests that the decision to include the H-bomb issue "profoundly affected the nature and conduct of the Oppenheimer Security Case."[2] Originally, the AEC commissioners had instructed Nichols to exclude the H-bomb controversy from his letter of derogatory information.[3] They feared public backlash if it appeared that Oppenheimer's *opinions* were on trial. However, on the afternoon of 13 December 1953, attorney Harold Green, Nichols's assistant, wrote a draft of the accusations that included the hydrogen bomb information. Since the commissioners' concern was that Oppenheimer's opinions not be challenged, Green wrote the section on the H-bomb decision with an emphasis on Oppenheimer's veracity. In fact, Green inserted the phrase, "your veracity, conduct, and even your loyalty" immediately after the H-bomb charges, in order to accentuate his particular terminological emphasis.[4]

The H-bomb evidence greatly influenced the hearing's terminology. First, it subtly interjected into the hearings the political battles in which Oppenheimer was embroiled, without explicitly challenging his right to an opinion. Second, it implicitly invoked a 1950s god-term, "progress" (of which Oppenheimer previously had been the ultimate symbol), *against* Oppenheimer. In equational form, the accusations stated that:

$$\text{Oppenheimer} = (-\text{anti-progress})$$

Weaver argued at the time that "progress" was "probably the only term which gave to the average American or West European . . . a concept of something bigger than himself, which he is socially impelled to accept and even to sacrifice for."[5] Weaver asserted further that "progress" was tied to humanity's relationship with nature. "Since the sixteenth century we have tended to accept as inevitable an historical development that takes the form of a changing relationship between ourselves and nature, in which we pass increasingly into the role of master of nature."[6] Consider Nichols's H-bomb charges in Weaver's terms. Oppenheimer allegedly had opposed hydrogen bomb development. He had stated that the knowledge of such a weapon, let alone its actual construction, should be avoided. In so many words, Oppenheimer argued that humankind should halt its growing control of the powerful forces of nature; he argued that, in effect, nuclear "progress" should stop. "Science," another god-term of the 1950s, was intertwined with "progress" in Oppenheimer's opinions. Oppenheimer not only thwarted progress, but he stood in the way of scientific and technological progress. He had come to stand in the way of the very thing that he most represented for many citizens. His equation was represented as:

$$\text{Oppenheimer} = (-\text{against scientific progress})$$

Thus, by including the H-bomb controversy in the letter of charges, Nichols could employ two concomitantly powerful, if implicit, terms against Oppenheimer: "science" and "progress."

Nichols's use of "un-American," "communist," and "scientific progress" to degrade Oppenheimer's position was especially effective because of the terms' interactions. Weaver submitted that the strength of terms like "the American way" rested in the implicit link between "progress" and "un-American" behavior. Writes Weaver:

"American" and "progressive" have an area of synonymity. The Western World had long stood as a symbol of the future; and accordingly, there has been a very wide tendency in this country, and also I believe among many people in Europe, to identify that which is American with that which is destined to be. And this is much the same as identifying it with the achievements of "progress."[7]

Oppenheimer was "un-American" not only in his associations, but also because he hindered, if only for a short time, America's destiny of nuclear superiority. In more global terms than were explicitly presented in the accusations, Oppenheimer's overall equation, according to Nichols, was:

Oppenheimer $= (-$communism$) + (-$against scientific progress$)$

The H-bomb evidence strengthened and unified Nichols's case. Had it not been included, the charges against Oppenheimer would have dealt primarily with Oppenheimer's 1930s left-wing associations. His advisory decisions and postwar activities might never have entered into the discussion.

A final observation rounds out evaluation of Nichols's strategic choices. He began a pattern in the case by which only negative information was considered. He did not quote the AEC security clearance guidelines, which recommended consideration of both favorable and unfavorable information and then an "overall commonsense judgment." Nichols created a list of particulars, all negative. He established an adversarial—actually oppositional—atmosphere, even though the proceedings, by definition, were an inquiry, not a trial. Nichols chose the parameters for discussion, highlighting only those rules likely to lead to Oppenheimer's defeat. Nichols established an offensive strategic posture for his rhetoric.

By accepting Nichols's parameters for argument—situating the dispute around character, associations, and loyalty—Oppenheimer filled the dialectical posture created for him by Nichols's position. Oppenheimer adopted a defensive stance; he accepted Nichols's terminology and acquiesced to his procedural norms.

Oppenheimer could have chosen more productive paths. As Philip Reif noted at the time, "his response to the rehash of his past in the charged climate of America was, if anything, too appropriate to the pattern of attack."[8] Had Oppenheimer followed precedent, he might have avoided the entire proceeding. In 1948 when Condon, the scientist that Gray and Morgan believed had "undue influence" over Oppenheimer, faced security problems similar to Oppenheimer's, he resigned to protest the government's harassment.[9] Haberer notes that "in contrast to Oppenheimer, Condon fought on his own behalf, in effect, if gestures have any meaning, he acted closely on the assumption that the government needed the scientists rather than the scientists needed government."[10]

Oppenheimer, however, had "made his mark" through government service, and perhaps resignation was inconceivable to him. Some of Oppenheimer's detractors felt that Oppenheimer, in particular, desired and needed the prestige lent by his advisory role. In 1943, one security official noted that "Oppenheimer was deeply concerned with gaining a worldwide reputation as a scientist, and a place in history."[11] Whatever his reasons, perhaps Oppenheimer's acceptance of Nichols's terminology was his greatest error. Oppenheimer did not quote the available documents to his advantage, and he centered his reply on explanations of the negative situations Nichols highlighted. He argued a case, the boundaries of which he allowed to be determined by Nichols.

Nichols had targeted Oppenheimer's most vulnerable points. Oppenheimer could not deny the charges. He had associated with Communists during the 1930s. Since Oppenheimer chose a defensive pattern, he was forced to explain his actions in complicated contextual terms. Despite the difficult political climate in 1954, Oppenheimer's explanation of his past associations was acceptable to both the Gray Board majority and the AEC majority. Both groups of judges agreed that Oppenheimer's past associations were of no present consequence. On the surface, this appears to have been Oppenheimer's most successful rhetorical strategy—yet recall that Oppenheimer argued that 1930s communist associations could not be considered fairly in the 1954 political context. This was implicit recognition that communist associations were unacceptable in 1954. Knowing this, perhaps Oppenheimer should never have touched the associations issue, since he could not truthfully deny current associations with Communists. He still considered Chevalier a friend, and had visited him only six months before the hearing began. Oppenheimer must also have realized that the FBI was thorough in its investigations; he had been followed, and his phones had been tapped, for over eleven years. There was no doubt that his recent visit to Chevalier was known to his judges. He could not avoid the "facts." Neither the Gray Board nor the AEC majority overlooked his continued communist associations. In both judgments, Oppenheimer's continued association with Chevalier was used against him.

Oppenheimer's reply to the H-bomb issue was faulty as well. He could easily have stated that his advisory opinions were simply "advice" and "opinions," to be considered and either accepted or rejected by those he advised. If his advice was unwelcome or erroneous, he could be fired; but his opinions were irrelevant to his security and his veracity. He need not have argued that the scientific advisor's role excluded political, military, or moral recommendations; this argument—advanced by Oppenheimer and adopted by Gray and Morgan—only weakened Oppenheimer's case.

Ironically, the AEC commissioners argued for Oppenheimer's right to his opinion even though Oppenheimer did not. Their argument, in the absence of any similar statement by Oppenheimer, suggests that Oppenheimer missed a vulnerable point in Nichols's use of the "progress" and "American" terminologies. Invocation of "freedom of speech," a potentially powerful terminological ally for Oppenheimer, might have been sufficient to "defuse" the entire H-bomb issue, or at least to better balance the poles of opposition.

Oppenheimer could also have used Nichols's terms against Nichols: to deny a citizen's right to an opinion, whether technical, political, ethical, or otherwise, is itself supposed to be "un-American." Oppenheimer's defense might have profited from use of these equations:

$$(+\text{scientific advisor's opinion}) = (+\text{free expression of ideas})$$

$$(\text{Oppenheimer's advice}) = (+\text{free expression of ideas})$$

$$(-\text{Nichols's charges}) = (-\text{against free expression})$$

$$(-\text{Nichols's charges}) = (-\text{un-American activity})$$

Oppenheimer could have extended this argument further through a redefinition of the scientific advisor's role in relation to his recommendations. All parties in the hearing agreed that a scientific advisor's work is to provide the best possible recommendation, given that person's understanding of the issues. Accordingly, Oppenheimer's argument might have followed these lines: Although he honestly believed otherwise, Oppenheimer could have told the AEC, the military, and others what he knew they wanted to hear. His advice would have been valued, and he probably would never have faced a Personnel Security Hearing. He had placed himself at risk in order to do what he believed was his patriotic duty—to provide the government with his best ideas and advice. To do any less would be a true threat to the national security. He could have argued that his critical and unpopular recommendations, made against high-powered adversaries, indicated a high sense of loyalty because of the risk he had incurred. He had placed the nation's interests ahead of his career and his personal reputation.

Unfortunately for Oppenheimer, he confined himself to a reactive posture and tried to counter Nichols's charges in Nichols's terms. Oppenheimer chose to discuss his loyalty to the security system and his organizational loyalty. This response accomplished two things. First, it opened the door for Gray and Morgan's discussion of Oppenheimer's lack of enthusiasm in H-bomb development. Second, it removed any possibility that Oppenheimer might challenge the implicit political motivations behind the entire case. Haberer argues that, once again, Oppenheimer actually aided his accusers:

Oppenheimer's unwillingness to choose a political terrain on which to defend himself abetted the government's unwillingness to examine openly the real ground for attacking him. The public thus never had the opportunity to examine the basic policy questions camouflaged by the deceptive security and loyalty issues. The open decision on his character masked the hidden decision on his policy.[12]

Oppenheimer himself made Nichols's H-bomb evidence viable. The AEC, however, guardedly dismissed the issue. Of course, according to procedure, the AEC would never have addressed the Oppenheimer case had the Personnel Security Board recommended reinstatement of Oppenheimer's security clearance. Once the AEC became involved, however, it did not need the H-bomb evidence to arrive at a negative security sum.

The AEC majority decision merely reiterated Nichols's original charges, except that it excluded the H-bomb controversy. Oppenheimer's character and associations were, for them, negative. The similarity is not surprising, since the commissioners had had final approval of the original accusations. Having found no sufficient evidence to the contrary, they merely restated a foregone conclusion: Oppenheimer was a security risk.

Nichols's terminological choices tapped the rhetorical resources of Oppenheimer's history and of the political and social climate of 1954. By choosing to follow Nichols's pattern, Oppenheimer failed to garner his own available, and not insubstantial, rhetorical resources. In his own defense, he adopted the Nichols terminology and gave the charges credence. He did not use his own status, his accomplishments, his political knowledge, the documented standards, or even his freedom of speech to his advantage. At the same time, as pointed out above, he interjected terms into the security equation that proved to be to his detriment. Whether or not the decision was predetermined, Oppenheimer did little to dissuade his accusers from their chosen path. Even Gray and Morgan, who appeared to hold Oppenheimer in high regard, felt compelled to agree with the Nichols accusations.

THEORETICAL LESSONS OF THE OPPENHEIMER CASE

On a broader theoretical level, the Oppenheimer case sheds light on the rhetorical interactions of accusations, defense strategies, and decision justifications.

First, note that a single piece of derogatory information, the Chevalier Incident, was used by Gray and Morgan to impugn Oppenheimer's "loyalty to the security system," by the AEC majority to degrade his "character," and by Murray to call Oppenheimer "disloyal." Here this case demonstrates both the importance of terminologies in constructing a meaningful interpretation of any situation and the rhetorical uses of evidence. Each judge applied a particular "frame of acceptance" to the "facts" and arrived at negative, but still qualitatively different, explanations of Oppenheimer's actions.

Second, the case clearly demonstrates the central role that ethical standards and criteria play in apologetic situations. Nichols molded the accusation, and eventually Oppenheimer's defense, by first making a strategic presentation of the AEC standards and then defining Oppenheimer's acts as violations of the standards as he presented them. Had Nichols emphasized an "overall commonsense judgment," as recommended elsewhere in the regulations, Oppenheimer's judges might have decided very differently. Whether the guideline is a legal statute, a political document, or a generally accepted societal standard, the evaluative criteria are a rhetorical resource for both the person making the accusation and the individual offering a defense.

Third, Oppenheimer's contextualization strategy is problematic in apologetic situations that deal not only with evaluation of past acts but measures of future trustworthiness. Trust is a measure of predictability. We trust someone who we know will act in particular positive ways at particular times. Oppenheimer's overall strategy, however, is based not on predictability but on human changeability. While many people who examine Oppenheimer's record might agree that he was more fit to serve government in 1954 than in 1945, they might also ask what "mistake" he would need to make next in his learning process. If a defense based on changing conditions and changing understanding is to encourage a judgment of trustworthiness by others, the rhetor must highlight the underlying principles that have guided the subject's decision and action through periods of change. Judges must be able to discern the fundamental values and beliefs that can be expected to lead the individual to make "right" decisions in future situations. Unfortunately for Oppenheimer, some of his judges failed to recognize such principles in his behavior, and others felt that Oppenheimer's principles were flawed.

Fourth, the Oppenheimer case demonstrates the multitude of possible explanations for action that exist in any situation and the role of rhetoric in creating and judging those explanations. Character cannot be seen or touched or measured in any direct way. Intentions may be expressed or discerned, but never proven. Actions are not merely facts; they are defined according to the observer's orientation to human motivation. Political persona are therefore created, and often transformed, through symbolic interaction.

POSTLUDE

Despite numerous biographies and analyses of the 1954 security hearing, only one official document interprets Oppenheimer's contributions to the U.S. government. The decisions found in the 1954 hearing transcript, whatever the procedural defense to the contrary, were "written," essentially, before the hearing began. From the start, Oppenheimer's case was legalistic, although it was not legal. Despite statements to the contrary and documented procedures that forbade a trial, the Oppenheimer case appears to have been adversarial from the start. A friend and consultant to Oppenheimer, Joseph Volpe, felt that the AEC began the proceedings with Oppenheimer's "conviction" as the goal. When the hearing began, Joseph Volpe suggested that Oppenheimer withdraw from the entire process.

It was clear from the way Robb [the government's attorney] was handling the case . . . that this was not an inquiry, but a prosecution. At that point I suggested to Robert that he tell the AEC to stick it, and just call the whole thing off, because then there wasn't the slightest doubt left that he was bound to go down.[13]

Oppenheimer, obviously, refused to withdraw. However, he also refused to fight effectively, using all available resources. Thereby, Oppenheimer became the government's strongest witness against himself. Not only did he adopt the AEC's rules and terminology, but in his response he did not even highlight the factors in his favor. Merely describing his contributions, Oppenheimer never stressed the brilliance of his service record—if anything, he played down his contributions to the government. Unlike Condon, Oppenheimer acted as if he dared not offend his accusers with a show of arrogance. Ironically, throughout his career, Oppenheimer had built a reputation for arrogance and persuasive brilliance; neither appeared in his defense.

Oppenheimer never pointed out that, security clearance or not, he knew all of the country's atomic secrets intimately. He did not need the AEC's classified material if he wanted to betray his country. Perhaps he thought that he need not remind the Gray Board or the AEC of his professional and public stature. Perhaps he thought that the government would not risk the adverse reaction of the public and of the scientific community by actually ruling against him.

If this was what Oppenheimer thought, he clearly was wrong. With the decision of 29 June 1954, Oppenheimer was permanently removed from public service. As a bitter and perhaps telling irony, his contract with the AEC would have expired the next day; no hearing was needed just to remove Oppenheimer from government service.

The matter of J. Robert Oppenheimer encapsulated much of the beginning drama of the nuclear age, when U.S. policymakers first felt the challenge and uncertainty of nuclear power, the power of nuclear knowledge, and the importance of risks to security. Scientists, while vital to the development of atomic weaponry, were not governed by a military system or even by a philosophy that matched the political arena. The investigation of Oppenheimer's life provided the means to establish such a standard; in effect, Oppenheimer's case was an inquiry into the first ten years of nuclear science in politics. Unfortunately, the Nichols accusations prevailed in the

Oppenheimer case, and a valuable source of knowledge and inspiration left the political arena. When the AEC removed Oppenheimer's security clearance, for some they transformed a hero into a villain; for others they made the hero into a martyr.

After the hearing, Oppenheimer, deeply affected by the decision, continued as director of the Institute for Advanced Study at Princeton and virtually disappeared from public life.

A Kennedy advisor later suggested that the case generated political problems for later administrations. "The case had given the U.S. a black eye among liberals and intellectuals abroad. It had caused this hurtful blood feud among American scientists and, besides, we felt it had been a tragic miscarriage of justice."[14] In 1963, as President Kennedy brought "intellectuals" into government service, he also took steps to rectify Oppenheimer's situation, some said to rehabilitate Oppenheimer. After he tested public reaction by inviting Oppenheimer to a White House dinner, Kennedy moved to reunite Oppenheimer with his government. The means to "rehabilitate" Oppenheimer was the Enrico Fermi Award, the highest honor bestowed by the AEC. As one of his last official acts, President Kennedy decided to present the award to Oppenheimer personally. However, when Oppenheimer received the award on 2 December 1963, exactly one decade after President Eisenhower ordered a blank wall placed between Oppenheimer and his government, it had to be President Johnson who presented the honor.

Oppenheimer's rehabilitation was not without echoes of the controversy that had ousted him. The Republican members of the Joint Atomic Energy Committee refused to attend the awards ceremony. Oppenheimer's words at the time reflect the political upheaval caused by the award: "I think it is possible, Mr. President, that it has taken some courage and some charity for you to make this award today."[15] After the award, Oppenheimer returned to private life.

Oppenheimer died on 18 February 1967. At the time of his death, Oppenheimer was still officially a "security risk." Although the agency that had removed Oppenheimer from government service later gave him its highest honor, Oppenheimer's reputation was never cleared. That would have required another security hearing, and Oppenheimer refused to open his life to yet another interpretation. The findings of the Personnel Security Board and the AEC recommendations, which rewrote Oppenheimer's life, remain intact. To this day, the transcript created in 1954 is the official record in the matter of J. Robert Oppenheimer.

NOTES

1. Richard M. Weaver, *The Ethics of Rhetoric* (Chicago: Henry Regnery, 1953), 219.

2. Philip M. Stern, *The Oppenheimer Case: Security on Trial* (New York: Harper and Row, 1969), 226.

3. Ibid., 225-26.

4. Ibid., 227.

5. Weaver, *Ethics of Rhetoric*, 214.

6. Ibid., 213.

7. Ibid., 218.

8. Philip Reif, "The Case of Dr. Oppenheimer," *Twentieth Century* 156 (1954): 222.

9. Joseph Haberer, *Politics and the Community of Science* (New York: Van Nostrand Reinhold, 1969), 246.

10. Ibid.

11. U.S. Atomic Energy Commission, *In the Matter of J. Robert Oppenheimer: Transcript of Hearing before Personnel Security Board* (Washington, D.C.: Government Printing Office, 1954), 275.

12. Haberer, *Politics*, 247.

13. Robert Coughlan, "The Tangled Drama and Private Hells of Two Famous Scientists," *Life*, 13 December 1963, 98.

14. Ibid., 110.

15. "Oppenheimer's Remarks," *New York Times*, 3 December 1963, A23.

Bibliography

PRIMARY DOCUMENTS

"Executive Order 10450. *Federal Register* 18 (1953): 2491.

U.S. Atomic Energy Commission, *In the Matter of J. Robert Oppenheimer: Texts of Principal Documents and Letters of Personnel Security Board, May 27, 1954, through June 19, 1954*. Washington, D.C.: Government Printing Office, 1954.

_____. *In the Matter of J. Robert Oppenheimer: Transcript of Hearing before Personnel Security Board*. Washington, D.C.: Government Printing Office, 1954.

_____. "Personnel Security Clearance Criteria for Determining Eligibility. *Federal Register* 15 (1950): 8094.

PRIMARY SOURCES

Abel, Elie. "Hydrogen Blast Astonished Scientists, Eisenhower Says." *New York Times*, 25 March 1954, A1.

_____. "2 H-Bomb Leaders at Odds over Oppenheimer Attitude." *New York Times*, 17 June 1954, A1.

"AEC Action against Oppenheimer Includes Old and New Charges." *Washington Post*, 14 April 1954, A2.

Alsop, Joseph, and Stewart Alsop. "Matter of Fact: Pandora's Box 1." *Washington Post*, 2 January 1950, A8.

_____. "Matter of Fact: They Can Do It Too." *Washington Post*, 6 January 1950, A21.

_____. "A Scientist under Probe in Security Case." *Washington Post*, 13 April 1954, A1.

"The Atom: Man in the Middle." *Newsweek*, 28 June 1954, 20.

"The Atom: The Road beyond Elugelab." *Time*, 12 April 1954, 22.

"The Atomic Age." *Time*, 29 October 1945, 30.

Baldwin, Hanson W. "Atom Tests Emphasize Stepped-up Arms Race: New Series in Pacific Will Include First Operating Model of H-Bomb." *New York Times*, 7 March 1954, D5.

_____. "Science Schism Widens: Oppenheimer Debate Impedes Progress in United States Military Technology." *New York Times*, 1 July 1954, A2.

Barnett, Lincoln. "J. Robert Oppenheimer." *Life*, 10 October 1949, 121.

Bethe, Hans. "The Hydrogen Bomb." *Bulletin of the Atomic Scientists* 6 (1950): 99-104.

"The Case of Robert Oppenheimer." *New Republic*, 26 April 1954, 15.

"Color Photographs Add Vivid Reality to Nation's Concept of H-Bomb." *Life*, 19 April 1954, 21-24.

Coughlan, Robert. "Dr. Edward Teller's Magnificent Obsession: Story behind the H-Bomb Is One of Dedicated, Patriotic Man Overcoming High-Level Opposition." *Life*, 6 September 1954, 61-74.

Davies, Lawrence E. " 'The Atom' on the Air." *New York Times*, 26 June 1955, B11.

Davis, Harry M. "The Man Who Built the A-Bomb." *New York Times Magazine*, 18 April 1948, 54.

"Did the Soviet Bomb Come Sooner Than Expected?" *Bulletin of the Atomic Scientists* 5 (1949): 262-64.

"Dr. Oppenheimer Discusses Future." *New York Times*, 4 July 1954, A15.

Editorial, "The Oppenheimer Case." *Bulletin of the Atomic Scientists* 10 (1954): 173.

Eisenhower, Dwight D. "The President's News Conferences of April 7, 1954." *Public Papers of the Presidents of the United States: Dwight D. Eisenhower, 1954*. Washington, D.C.: Government Printing Office, 1955.

_____. "Radio and Television Address to the American People on the State of the Nation." *Public Papers of the Presidents of the United States: Dwight D. Eisenhower, 1954*. Washington, D.C.: Government Printing Office, 1955.

"Eisenhower Releases Movie of Superbomb." *New York Times*, 27 March 1954, A1.

"The Eternal Apprentice." *Time*, 8 November 1948, 70.

"Ex-Member of AEC Backs Oppenheimer." *Washington Post*, 14 April 1954, A2.

"Fight That Held Up the H-Bomb: The Real Story behind the Delay." *U.S. News and World Report*, 16 April 1954, 35.

"Fisherman Burned in Bikini Test Blast." *New York Times*, 16 March 1954, A19.

"5-4-3-2-1 and the Hydrogen Age Is upon Us." *Life*, 12 April 1954, 24-32.

"4-Year H-Bomb Lag Laid to Oppenheimer; His Counsel Says He Is Not a Security Risk; Teller, Hydrogen Pioneer, Charges Physicist Gave No Moral Support." *New York Times*, 16 June 1954, A1.

"Groves Backs His Selection of Oppenheimer for A-Post." *Washington Post*, 4 April 1954, A2.

"The Hidden Struggle for the H-Bomb: The Story of Dr. Oppenheimer's Persistent Campaign to Reverse the U.S. Military Strategy." *Fortune*, May 1953, 109-10.

"How U.S. Almost Lost the Atom Race: Heels Dragged after 1945—Russia Pushed Ahead." *U.S. News and World Report*, 25 June 1954, 24-27.

"Hydrogen Bomb Confirmed." *New York Times*, 17 March 1954, A9.

"Ike Bars A-Secrets from Oppenheimer." *Washington Post*, 14 April 1954, A15.

"J. Robert Oppenheimer: His Life & Times." *Time*, 26 April 1954, 19-22.

Kalven, Harry, Jr. "The Case of J. Robert Oppenheimer before the Atomic Energy Commission." *Bulletin of the Atomic Scientists* 10 (1954): 259-69.

Laurence, William L. "Much Hydrogen Bomb Data Known; Process Involves Fusion of Atoms." *New York Times*, 18 January 1950, A13.

_____. "Teller Indicates Reds Gain on Bomb: Soviets Came Close to Beating U.S. to First Superweapon, He Says in Interview." *New York Times*, 4 July 1954, A15.

_____. "12 Physicists Ask U.S. Not to Be First to Use Super Bomb." *New York Times*, 5 February 1950, A1.

_____. "Vast Power Bared: March 1 Explosion Was Equivalent to Millions of Tons of TNT." *New York Times*, 1 April 1954, A1.

Lavine, Harold. "H–Mystery Man: He Hurried the H-Bomb." *Newsweek*, 2 August 1954, 23-26.

Lee, James. "Oppenheimer Role in H-Program Sifted." *Washington Post*, 13 April 1954, A2.

"The Man Who Made the Bomb." *Newsweek*, 10 May 1982, 65.

Martin, Dwight. "First Casualties of the H-Bomb." *Life*, 29 March 1954, 17-21.

"New and Mightier Atom Smasher." *Life*, 12 April 1954, 62-66.

"No Revolt among Scientists: Thousands Are Hard at Work on Atomic Jobs." *U.S. News and World Report*, 30 April 1954, 30.

"Open Letter to President Eisenhower." *Bulletin of the Atomic Scientists* 10 (1954): 283.

Oppenheimer, J. Robert. "The Atom Bomb as a Great Force for Peace." *New York Times Magazine*, 9 June 1946, 7.

"The Oppenheimer Case." *Physics Today* 7 (1954): 7.

"The Oppenheimer Paradox: Sense and Senselessness." *Newsweek*, 26 April 1954, 28-29.

"The Oppenheimer Story." *Time*, 26 April 1954, 69.

People of the Week." *U.S. News and World Report*, 25 June 1954, 16.

"Read the Oppenheimer Transcript." *Bulletin of the Atomic Scientists* 10 (1954): 258.

Reston, James. "Dr. Oppenheimer Suspended by A.E.C. in Security Review; Scientist Defends Record." *New York Times*, 13 April 1954, A1.

Ryan, Edward F. "Oppenheimer Hearing Record Reveals Battle over Security Gain or Loss." *Washington Post*, 17 June 1954, A11.

Sawyer, Roland. "More than Security." *Bulletin of the Atomic Scientists* 10 (1954): 284.

"Scientists Affirm Faith in Oppenheimer." *Bulletin of the Atomic Scientists* 10 (1954): 188.

"Scientists Are Disappointed." *New York Times*, 30 June 1954, A10.

"Scientists Express Confidence in Oppenheimer." *Bulletin of the Atomic Scientists* 10 (1954): 283.

"2nd Hydrogen Blast Proves Mightier Than Any Forecast." *New York Times*, 18 March 1954, A1.

"Secrets Will Out." *Bulletin of the Atomic Scientists* 6 (1950): 67-68.

"Security or Sterility?" *Washington Post*, 14 April 1954: A14.

Shepley, James R., and Clay Blair, Jr. "Inside Story of the Hydrogen Bomb: How the U.S. Almost Lost It." *U.S. News and World Report*, 24 September 1954, 58.

Shils, Edward. "A Slippery Slope." *Bulletin of the Atomic Scientists* 10 (1954): 242.

"Teller, Hydrogen Pioneer, Charges Physicist Gave No Moral Support." *New York Times*, 16 June 1954, A1.

"Text of Statement and Comments by Strauss on Hydrogen Bomb Tests in the Pacific." *New York Times*, 1 April 1954, A20.

"Texts of Letter from A.E.C. General Manager to Dr. Oppenheimer and Scientist's Reply." *New York Times*, 13 April 1954, A16-18.

"The Thinkers: The Institute for Advanced Study Is Their Haven." *Life*, 29 December 1947, 58.

"U.S. Ponders a Scientist's Past." *Life*, 26 April 1954, 35.

"What Is a Security Risk?" *Bulletin of the Atomic Scientists* 10 (1954): 241.

"What the Scientists Are Saying." *Bulletin of the Atomic Scientists* 6 (1950): 71-75.

SECONDARY SOURCES

Ames, Mary E. *Outcome Uncertain: Science and the Political Process*. Washington, D.C.: Communications Press, 1978.

Cox, Donald W. *America's New Policy Makers: The Scientists' Rise to Power*. New York: Chilton, 1964.

Curtis, Charles P. *The Oppenheimer Case: Trial of a Security System*. New York: Simon and Schuster, 1955.

Davis, Nuel Pharr. *Lawrence and Oppenheimer*. 1968. Reprint. New York: Da Capo, 1986.

Dupré, J. Stephan, and Sanford A. Lakoff. *Science and the Nation: Policy and Politics*. Englewood Cliffs, N.J.: Prentice-Hall, 1962.

Gilman, William. *Science, U.S.A.* New York: Viking, 1967.

Gilpin, Robert. *American Scientists and Nuclear Weapons Policy*. Princeton, N.J.: Princeton University Press, 1962.

Goodchild, Peter. *J. Robert Oppenheimer: Shatterer of Worlds*. Boston: Houghton Mifflin, 1981.

Haberer, Joseph. *Politics and the Community of Science*. New York: Van Nostrand Reinhold, 1969.

Jungk, Robert. *Brighter than a Thousand Suns: A Personal History of the Atomic Scientists*. New York: Harcourt, Brace, 1958.

Kunetka, James W. *Oppenheimer: The Years of Risk*. Englewood Cliffs, N.J.: Prentice-Hall, 1982.

Lapp, Ralph E. *The New Priesthood: The Scientific Elite and the Uses of Power*. New York: Harper and Row, 1965.

Major, John. *The Oppenheimer Hearing*. New York: Stein and Day, 1971.

Michelmore, Peter. *The Swift Years: The Robert Oppenheimer Story*. New York: Dodd, Mead, 1969.

Newhouse, John. *War and Peace in the Nuclear Age*. New York: Knopf, 1989.

Nieburg, H. L. *In the Name of Science*. Chicago: Quadrangle, 1966.

Pfau, Richard. *No Sacrifice Too Great: The Life of Lewis L. Strauss*. Charlottesville: University Press of Virginia, 1984.

Price, Donald K. *The Scientific Estate*. Cambridge: Belknap, 1967.

Rhodes, Richard. *The Making of the Atomic Bomb.* New York: Simon and Schuster, 1986.

Rosenberg, David Alan. "American Atomic Strategy and the Hydrogen Bomb Decision." *Journal of American History* 66 (1979): 62-87.

Royal, Denise. *The Story of J. Robert Oppenheimer.* New York: St. Martin's, 1969.

Smith, Alice Kimball. *A Peril and a Hope: The Scientists' Movement in America: 1945-1947.* Chicago: University of Chicago Press, 1965.

Smith, Alice Kimball, and Charles Wiener, eds. *Robert Oppenheimer: Letters and Recollections.* Cambridge: Harvard University Press, 1980.

Stein, Jonathan B. *From H-Bomb to Star Wars.* Washington, D.C.: Lexington, 1984.

Stern, Philip M. *The Oppenheimer Case: Security on Trial.* New York: Harper and Row, 1969.

Sylves, Richard T. *The Nuclear Oracles: A Political History of the General Advisory Committee of the Atomic Energy Commission, 1947-1977.* Ames: Iowa State University Press, 1987.

Weart, Spencer R. *Nuclear Fear: A History of Images.* Cambridge: Harvard University Press, 1988.

Williams, Robert C., and Philip L. Cantelon, eds. *The American Atom: A Documentary History of Nuclear Policies from the Discovery of Fission to the Present, 1939-1984.* Philadelphia: University of Pennsylvania Press, 1984.

Wilson, Thomas W., Jr. *The Great Weapons Heresy.* Boston: Houghton Mifflin, 1970.

Wyden, Peter. *Day One: Before Hiroshima and After.* New York: Warner, 1984.

York, Herbert. *The Advisors: Oppenheimer, Teller, and the Superbomb.* San Francisco: W. H. Freeman, 1976.

THEORETICAL AND METHODOLOGICAL SOURCES

Berthold, Carol A. "Kenneth Burke's Cluster-Agon Method: Its Development and an Application." *Central States Speech Journal* 17 (1976): 302-9.

Bostdorff, Denise M. " 'The Decision Is Yours' Campaign: Planned Parenthood's Character-istic Argument of Moral Virtue." In Elizabeth L. Toth and Robert L. Heath, eds., *Rhetorical and Critical Approaches to Public Relations*, 301-13. Hillsdale, N.J.: Lawrence Erlbaum, 1992.

Brummett, Barry. "A Pentadic Analysis of Ideologies in Two Gay Rights Controversies." *Central States Speech Journal* 30 (1979): 250-61.

––––––. "Presidential Substance: The Address of August 15, 1973." *Western Journal of Speech Communication* 39 (1975): 249-59.

Burke, Kenneth. *Counter-Statement.* Berkeley: University of California Press, 1968.

––––––. *A Grammar of Motives.* Reprint of 1945 edition. Berkeley: University of California Press, 1969.

––––––. *Language as Symbolic Action: Essays on Life, Literature, and Method.* Berkeley: University of California Press, 1966.

––––––. "The Party Line." *Quarterly Journal of Speech* 62 (1976): 66.

––––––. *Permanence and Change: An Anatomy of Purpose.* 3d ed. Berkeley: University of California Press, 1984.

––––––. *The Philosophy of Literary Form.* 3d ed. Berkeley: University of California Press, 1973.

_____. *A Rhetoric of Motives*. Berkeley: University of California Press, 1969.

_____. "The Rhetorical Situation." In Lee Thayer, ed., *Communication: Ethical and Moral Issues*, 263-75. New York: Gordon and Breach Science, 1973.

_____. *Towards a Better Life: Being a Series of Epistles or Declamations*. Berkeley: University of California Press, 1966.

Crable, Richard E. "Ethical Codes, Accountability, and Argumentation." *Quarterly Journal of Speech* 64 (1978): 23-32.

Crowell, Laura. "Three Sheers for Kenneth Burke." *Quarterly Journal of Speech* 63 (1977): 152-77.

Frank, Armin Paul. *Kenneth Burke*. New York: Twayne, 1969.

Kruse, Noreen Wales. "Apologia in Team Sport." *Quarterly Journal of Speech* 67 (1981): 270-83.

_____. "Motivational Factors in Non-Denial Apologia." *Central States Speech Journal* 28 (1977): 13-23.

_____. "The Scope of Apologetic Discourse: Establishing Generic Parameters." *Southern Speech Communication Journal* 46 (1981): 278-91.

Mechling, Elizabeth Walker, and Jay Mechling. "Sweet Talk: The Moral Rhetoric against Sugar." *Central States Speech Journal* 34 (1983): 19-32.

Rueckert, William H. *Kenneth Burke and the Drama of Human Relations*. 2d ed. Berkeley: University of California Press, 1982.

Ryan, Halford Ross, ed. *Oratorical Encounters: Selected Studies and Sources of Twentieth-Century Political Accusations and Apologies*. New York: Greenwood, 1988.

Vibbert, Candiss Baksa. "The Supreme Court and Obscenity: The Judicial Opinion as Rhetorical Reconstitution." Ph.D. diss., University of Iowa, 1981.

Ware, B. L., and Wil Linkugel. "They Spoke in Defense of Themselves: On the Generic Criticism of Apologia." *Quarterly Journal of Speech* 59 (1973): 273-83.

Weaver, Richard M. *The Ethics of Rhetoric*. Chicago: Henry Regnery, 1953.

Index

About the Author

RACHEL L. HOLLOWAY is an Assistant Professor of Communication Studies at Virginia Polytechnic Institute and State University. Her research explores the area of issue management, especially the role that scientists and science play in the formation and justification of public policy in America.